Tune I
On, and Bliss Out

CW00417935

By

Sankarshan Das Adhikari

Dedicated to ISKCON

Founder - Acharya:

His Divine Grace *A.C. Bhaktivedanta Swami Prabhupada*

Srila Prabhupada Vyas Puja Homage for 2022

My Dear most beloved spiritual master, Srila Prabhupada,

Please accept my humble obeisances in the dust of your lotus feet.

In 1971 when I was a young newly initiated disciple you gave me the most wonderful following instruction in a letter from London dated 7 September 1971:

"I can see also that you are a very sincere and enthusiastic boy and are anxious for spreading this movement. Those are first class qualifications for making advancement in

Krishna Consciousness. So continue enthusiastically as you are doing and Krishna will surely bless you. "

This instruction is just as potent now as it was a half a century ago. Srila Prabhupada, you have written that the spiritual master lives forever by his divine instructions and the follower lives with him. So by embracing this order as my very life and soul you are personally present with me at every moment guiding me through all the difficulties of being Krishna conscious and empowering me to make a difference in this hellish material world.

Thank you, Srila Prabhupada, for being present me and guiding me how to be Krishna conscious.

Your lowly servant,

Sankarshan Das Adhikari

21.05.2022

CONTENT TABLE

INTRODUCTION

~~~ ~~~ ~~~

In this Krishna consciousness process, which is the highest perfection of the self-realization science, we teach you how to tune your mind into Krishna, the Supreme Personality of Godhead, the source of all existence; how to turn on your factual identity as His eternal servant; and how to thus totally transform your life into an ever-increasingly ecstatic celebration of transcendental bliss. This is more valuable than all of the wealth of this world multiplied by millions and billions of times. If you are ready for it now, we will give it to you. -July 29, 2019-

AUTHOR'S WORD

~~~ ~~~ ~~~

Sankarshan das Adhikari (SDA): Established by Srila Prabhupada, we are very much indebted to him for giving us the Bhagavatam and giving us this program to study a verse every day like this. It is very powerful, very ecstatic, very enlivening, very purifying, very uplifting, very enlightening experience to study Bhaktivedanta Purports to the Srimad Bhagavatam.

Lesson 1

QUALIFY TO GET OUT OF THE PRISON

~~~ ~~~ ~~~

Srimad Bhagavatam 3.29.44

Austin, Texas

Date: 21-FEB-2021

Om Namo Bhagavate Vasudevaya

[Gurudeva sings three times and devotees repeat]

*guṇābhimānino devāḥ
sargādiṣv asya yad-bhayāt
vartante 'nuyugaṁ yeṣāṁ
vaśa etac carācaram*

Synonyms

guṇa — the modes of material nature; *abhimāninaḥ* — in charge of; *devāḥ* — the demigods; *sarga-ādiṣu* — in the matter of creation and so on; *asya* — of this world; *yat-bhayāt* — out of fear of whom; *vartante* — carry out functions; *anuyugam* — according to the *yugas*; *yeṣām* — of whom; *vaśe* — under the control; *etat* — this; *cara-acaram* — everything animate and inanimate.

Translation

"Out of fear of the Supreme Personality of Godhead, the directing demigods in charge of the modes of material nature carry out the functions of creation, maintenance and destruction; everything animate and inanimate within this material world is under their control."

Purport

The three modes of material nature, namely goodness, passion and ignorance, are under the control of three deities — Brahma, Visnu and Lord Siva. Lord Viṣṇu is in charge of the mode of goodness, Lord Brahma is in charge of the mode of passion, and Lord Siva is in charge of the mode of ignorance. Similarly, there are many other demigods in charge of the air department, the water department, the cloud department, etc. Just as the government has many different departments, so, within this material world, the government of the Supreme Lord has many departments, and all these departments function in proper order out of fear of the Supreme Personality of Godhead. Demigods are undoubtedly controlling all matter, animate and inanimate, within the universe, but above them the supreme controller is the Personality of Godhead. Therefore in the *Brahma-samhita* it is said, *isvarah paramah Krsnah*. Undoubtedly there are many controllers in the departmental management of this universe, but the supreme controller is Krishna.

There are two kinds of dissolutions. One kind of dissolution takes place when Brahma goes to sleep during his night, and the final dissolution takes place when Brahma dies. As long as Brahma does not die, creation, maintenance and destruction are actuated by different demigods under the superintendence of the Supreme Lord. (End of Purport)

Sankarshan das Adhikari (SDA):

Even though there are many different departments – the rain department, the sun department, the vegetation department, the snake department, the rabbit department or porcupine department, the cactus department, so many departments. The Supreme Controller is ultimately behind everything. *isvarah paramah krsnah*. In India, many people worship different demigods – this demigod, that demigod, worship to get this thing, to get that thing, but this is less intelligence. Those who are less intelligent worship the demigods. Of course, they are better off than atheists, at least they understand there is some Supreme. They don't think they are the Supreme controllers. They are higher than the atheists. Foolish atheists will say that everything came out of nothing, but nothing comes out of nothing. These demigod worshippers are better than the atheists but still they are less intelligent because they do not see the Supreme Controller behind everything. What is the advantage of seeing the Supreme Controller behind everything? You may worship some demigod and get some temporary benefit but even the demigod is subject to laws of birth, death, old age and disease. The demigods are still within the material world. Even though they are on the higher planets but these higher planets are also destroyed at the time when Maha-Vishnu inhales, the whole universe is destroyed. The demigods may have very nice planets in the heavenly regions, a very long duration of life, but even they will also die. As long as you remain simply a demigod worshipper, worshipping the different departmental heads, you are worshipping those who are mortal, that means you will also remain mortal. If you worship the immortal, Supreme Personality of Godhead, Sri Krishna, Bhagavan, the source of all existence (BG 10.8) –

> *ahaṁ sarvasya prabhavo*
> *mattaḥ sarvaṁ pravartate*
> *iti matvā bhajante māṁ*
> *budhā bhāva-samanvitāḥ*

If you worship that Supreme Person who is the source of all existence, who is immortal, then you achieve your original identity of immortality. Actually, we are immortal beings. But only out of foolishness, out of our stupid desire to try to enjoy separately from the Lord, we have come to this place to try to do that and we are suffering like anything here. Specially recently, in Austin, we are suffering like anything. This is a foolish desire to try to enjoy separately from Krishna. Those who are intelligent, either through material science or through demigod worship, instead of trying to make better arrangements here, get out of this place. This is a prison. Do you want to remain in the prison and try to make nice arrangements in the prison?

What kind of intelligence is that? The prisoner is thinking, "O this prison is very nice, I will make nice arrangements,

I will bribe the guard, I will do so many things, I will make nice arrangements here to be happy." What kind of stupidity is that to remain in the prison? The intelligent person will say "Let me qualify to get out of this place. Let me learn how to abide by the laws of the government very nicely, so I become released, I became a free citizen once again." In the same way there is the Supreme government of Krishna. Instead of trying to defy the authority of Krishna and be thrown into this prison house of material existence, those who are intelligent, they say "Let me find out what Krishna wants." God is the law. His word is law. Why don't you find out what God wants? Is it difficult to do that? No. If you desire to find out what God wants, it is very simple. It's right here in the Bhagavad Gita. Simply study the Bhagavad Gita. You will understand exactly what God wants (BG 9.26) –

> *patraṁ puṣpaṁ phalaṁ toyaṁ*
> *yo me bhaktyā prayacchati*
> *tad ahaṁ bhakty-upahṛtam*
> *aśnāmi prayatātmanaḥ*

"If you will offer Me with love and devotion a leaf, a flower, fruit or water, I will accept it." Before you eat, you offer your food to Krishna. You can be a vegetarian, it's better than eating meat, but it's still sinful. Even eating vegetables, you get karma. If you don't offer the vegetables to Krishna, you will get karma because you are responsible for killing a living entity and eating it; if you didn't offer it to Krishna. We have to learn how to follow the instructions of Krishna. It's so nice thing. You can have a deity or put a nice picture of Krishna, set up a nice altar in your home, even a nice picture of Radha and Krishna there. You can put Prabhupada, you can put Bhakti Siddhanta Sarasvati Thakura, you can put Gaura Nitai, make a nice altar. And when you are initiated, you put your Spiritual Master also. You make a nice altar and get a really nice plate as Krishna's plate with some nice bowls, some spoons, put nice things, you can offer to Krishna and keep it in very nice condition, not dirty, rusty, nice and shiny, clean and make a very nice offering to the King and Queen of all existences. Why not serve the Supreme Lord and His eternal consort every time you eat? First serve Them. Feed Them. Cook for Krishna, make a nice offering for Krishna, in this way your eating should be centered around Krishna. And instead of talking nonsense, talk about Krishna. Talk about how Krishna swallowed that forest fire amazingly. Can you imagine there was whole forest fires, the Vrajavasis, were completely in anxiety. The cows and calves, everybody was completely bewildered and Krishna just (sound of swallowing) swallowed the forest fire. That's not an ordinary cowherd boy. Here He is playing as a simple cowherd boy then He swallows the forest fire. Such an amazing person. You can talk about His amazing pastimes, how He lifted the Govardhan. How Balarama was carried away by the demon Pralambhasura and He simply smashed Him on the head and killed Him immediately. There are so many amazing pastimes about Krishna and wonderful teachings of Krishna, Bhagavad Gita 18.66.

sarva-dharmān parityajya
mām ekaṁ śaraṇaṁ vraja

aham tvāṁ sarva-pāpebhyo
mokṣayiṣyāmi mā śucaḥ

We have to do everything we can, to be Krishna conscious. It's a difficult age. It's the age of Kali. 5,000 years ago, the age of Kali entered. Maharaj Parikshit was a very powerful king. By his influence Kali could not enter. Personality of Kali means you will have illicit sex, meat eating, intoxication and gambling. Of course, now it is everywhere, in every town, every village and every home, it is going on – illicit sex, meat eating, intoxication and gambling.

But 5000 years ago, Maharaj Parikshit, a very powerful devotee was able to hold off the age of Kali. But now we are in a very difficult situation. Everywhere this nonsense is going on.

Even our devotees are having difficulty sometimes in following the regulative principles. How do you become strong to not fall into this illicit sex? It's a big problem amongst our devotees. How do you become strong to protect yourself from these things? Well, you have to be Krishna conscious, the higher taste. There is a verse in the Gita about higher taste. ***Param dristva nivartate..***

We have to get the higher taste, that is the point. You have to practice Krishna consciousness in such a way that you get taste. Don't do mechanically. "I have this duty; I have to chant Hare Krishna Hare Krishna…"

Take this as special mercy from Srila Prabhupada, just like you are drowning in the ocean and somebody comes by in a ship and throw you a lifebuoy. He says, "Grab hold of this." You say, "What is this mechanical. I don't feel like grabbing onto it." No. "Wow! this is mercy!" Not that, "This is too much work grabbing onto this lifebuoy. I don't want to hold onto it. It's too much work." No, its special mercy. This lifebuoy is thrown to you. This is the loving kindness of some person on the ship. Hold on, they want to pull you in. Similarly this is great mercy of Srila Prabhupada, Srila Bhakti Siddhanta Sarasvati Thakura, of the Vaishnava preachers. They want to rescue you. They want to save you from the material existence. They may ask you to do something. All they are really saying is to hold onto the lifebuoy. That is all they are really saying. They are not trying to torture you or force you to do this and that. No. They are just saying to hold onto the lifebuoy, grab on and you are going to be pulled in. That's all we have to do. We have our regulative principles – no illicit sex, no meat eating, no intoxication and no gambling. You follow those, then you drive away Kali. If you engage in any of these things - illicit sex, meat eating, intoxication and gambling, Kali is sitting right there in your heart; you are tied and handcuffed by Kali. You are completely his prisoner. You kick away Kali. No illicit sex, no intoxication, no meat eating and no gambling. "Kali, get out of here and don't ever come back again." If you do that then you can peacefully chant – *Hare Krishna Hare Krishna Krishna Krishna Hare Hare, Hare Rama Hare Rama Rama Rama Hare Hare*, diving deeper & deeper into Nama ruci. Actually, we talk about going back to home, back to Godhead, we can be with Krishna, Gopis, the cowherd boys, the cowherd girls, you know what? You don't have to wait. You can be with Krishna right now, packed up tightly with Krishna, because He has come as Nama avatar. He is fully present in ***Hare Krishna Hare Krishna Krishna Krishna Hare Hare, Hare Rama Hare Rama Rama Rama Hare Hare***. Krishna is fully present right here right now. We don't have to think about dying and going back to Godhead and be with Krishna. You can be with Krishna right now, just give up illicit sex, meat eating, intoxication and gambling, sincerely try to avoid the 10 offences and just chant Hare Krishna with full absorption and you will be in direct contact with the Supreme Lord. Your Japa period will be like you are right there in Goloka Vrindavan with Radha and Krishna. If you are really in your japa, you will be in Goloka Vrindavan with Radha and Krishna right there in the middle of Their pastimes. ***Hare Krishna Hare Krishna Krishna Krishna Hare Hare, Hare Rama Hare Rama Rama Rama Hare Hare.*** And the material world will be far, far away from you. And at the same time, your pure chanting will have a very powerful uplifting impact on the material world. Even Prabhupada says amazingly that "if one chants the Holy Names of the Lord purely, then by his influence the whole world will chant Hare Krishna." There is a great opportunity we have for our own liberation and the libération of the fallen souls just by the quality of how we chant Hare Krishna. Take the quality of your chanting very very seriously and then the expansion of your chanting is your service. How do you do your service, do you do it grudgingly or you do it sincerely, do the best you possibly can? Sometimes we neophytes, we have this tendency, "I don't feel like doing it. Let me get this half done and get out of here and go sleep." Sometimes we neophytes have this tendency. We neophyte devotees suffer by holding onto that kind of consciousness. "I will do halfway and get out of here as fast as I can, so I can go sleep or go space out on the internet. This is nonsense. We neophyte devotees have to come out of this neophyte platform and become very serious to become pure devotees, in everything we do at every minute, 24/7 with every thought, every word and every deed completely absorbed in Krishna consciousness and no more spacing out in the material energy or spacing out in the mode of ignorance, or in the mode of passion. We have to become serious about this and stop being such knuckleheads, dull headed fools and rascals. Prabhupada said "Don't be a lazy fellow." Stop being so lazy, not wanting to do any devotional service, just wanting to be spaced out, overeat, oversleep etc. etc. etc. It's time to become very serious about kicking Kali out. As long as we indulge in these laziness and craziness, means we are still captured by Kali. We have to kick out Kali. We want to actually associate with Krishna, we actually want to be with Krishna, we actually want to relish the association of Krishna. We actually want to make a spiritual revolution on this planet to make the whole Krishna conscious as Prabhupada ordered us, we have to become free from the influence of Kali, free from the influence of *tamo guna*, free from the influence of *rajo guna.*

It's easy to say these things but for some of us, it's not so easy to practice it. But by meditating on it, and begging Krishna, "My dear Lord, mostly I am a *tamo guni*, sometimes a little *rajo guni*, hardly any *sattva guna.* I am in a very fallen position. I get overwhelmed by anger, I get overwhelmed by lust, I get overwhelmed by greed, I have all these bad qualities my dear Lord, I am just begging You – please save me from this horrible position I am in. Here I am trying to be a devotee, but I can't even control my senses. My dear Lord, I hear that You are *Hrsikesa,* the master of the senses, my dear Lord, **Hrsikena hrsikesa-sevanam**, I am begging You my dear Lord, please engage these rascal senses 100% in Your service. Get me out of Maya. Please Krishna, save me from horrible Maya that I am in."

In this way we have to beg Krishna and Krishna will reciprocate. If we are sincerely begging Krishna to save us from this Maya that we are in, He will. Krishna will liberate us. He wants us to be back in pure devotional service. He doesn't want us to be suffering here in this cycle of birth and death. He wants us to be back with Him in the spiritual world engaged in our original relationship in any one of the 5 primary rasas, as conjugal relationship, parental relationship, fraternal relationship, servitor relationship or neutral relationship. Each one of us has an eternal relationship with Krishna in any one of these 5 primary rasas. And Krishna wants to have us back. He is missing us like anything. He wants to have us back in our original relationship that we have with Him but we ran away from Him trying to enjoy separately. In this way, we have to become very serious now to understand the Supreme Personality of Godhead, who is the source of all existence, Bhagavan. He has all power, all beauty, all renunciation, all knowledge, all wealth and all fame. That's why He is called Bhagavan. "*Bhaga*" means "opulence". There are 6 opulences – power, beauty, renunciation, knowledge, wealth and fame. Every one of these things is an opulence. If someone is very powerful, it's a great opulence, like president of United States, very powerful person or big General or some heavy-duty wrestler who can defeat everyone. Just like our Jayapataka Swami, in his earlier days, he was a powerful wrestler. Some devotees came from Japan, very fired up *brahmacaris,* they would have wrestling matches on the bank of the Yamuna. They had the biggest wrestler who could defeat everybody but Jayapataka just threw him on the ground, boom. Of course, now he is, in an old man's body but he had the opulence of being very very powerful physically, in his early days in Mayapur. Even before we had any buildings, there were snakes over there, it was very wild in those early days in Mayapur. There was only one building, that was it. For the devotees there were no proper toilets, no proper showers, very, very austere, but these devotees were very dedicated. Jayapataka was known for being very powerful, he had the opulence of power. And beauty, of course our ladies in ISKCON are very beautiful but they are nothing compared to the beauty of Krishna. Krishna is unlimitedly beautiful. That's why He is called all-attractive. He is more beautiful than anything and everything. Someone is very beautiful, they are very attractive, Miss Universe or Miss America, so-called beauties, but Krishna surpasses in all of these beauties. If someone is very renounced, they are considered very opulent. Because, multi-billionaire, is considered very attractive, if somebody is very knowledgeable, has a PhD degree, is considered very attractive. All these things are considered very attractive – Power, beauty, renunciation, knowledge, wealth and fame. But that person who has unlimited power, unlimited beauty, unlimited renunciation, unlimited knowledge, unlimited wealth and unlimited fame, that person is Bhagavan, the possessor of all opulences and that is Krishna. Actually the whole world will become attracted to Krishna; we just have to introduce them to Krishna. Right now, they are running after the movie stars, the rock stars, the porno queens or whatever, they are running after all these nonsense people. According to their different modes, they are running here, running there, attracted to this, attracted to that – The rock stars, the movie stars, all political stars, the fighting heroes, they are all running after these personalities but Krishna, He is all powerful, all beautiful, all renounced, all wise, all famous, all wealthy, if they can actually understand who is Krishna, the whole world will run after Krishna. This is our goal in Krishna consciousness movement. We want to make the whole world Krishna conscious, to save these people from their horrible sufferings in the cycle of birth and death. We are praying to Krishna, "Please Krishna bless us that we can now make the whole world Krishna conscious. As soon as possible put a stop to all the sufferings of these people, put a stop to these slaughterhouses, abortion clinics, gay marriages, this nonsense is going on, we want to stop all this and bring Vedic culture back to this planet, so we can have sanity on this planet once again. That means we have to cooperate. That's how we will have strength in our movement, by cooperating. Just like the British had a very tightknit cooperation, because of that they had a huge empire all over the world, of course it's fallen apart now because it was not based on Krishna. Because they were very cooperative amongst themselves, they had a very tiny island but then they had a huge empire all over the whole world, by the tightknit cooperation with each other. We should learn from that example. We should have very tight-knit cooperation within ISKCON. In this way we can conquer the world if we have a very tight-knit cooperation with each other. In this way, we should learn as a very tightknit doing things as a team to cooperate with each other to serve Srila Prabhupada's instructions. We want the whole world to be happy and we have the formula how to do it. Now we have to faithfully follow the instructions of His Divine Grace Srila Prabhupada and the most amazing future awaits us.

Questions & Answers:

Bahurupa Caitanya das: What is the key to become successful spiritual practitioner?

SDA: Sincerity is the key, Bahurupa Caitanya Das. Sincerity is the key. You have to be sincere. You have to realize that there is no real alternative. Become Krishna conscious or suffer like hell. One has to understand there is really no alternative. Proper understanding should be there and then you should sincerely try to become Krishna's pure devotee. You should become qualified as Prabhupada told me, "Now you just become qualified to see Krishna face to face." That means to be a completely pure devotee. You should aspire to become a completely pure devotee, Bahurupa Caitanya Das, completely free from lust, anger, greed, madness, illusion, envy, laziness and craziness, completely pure devotee. You should beg Krishna. "My dear Krishna, please bless me that I can be Your pure devotee. Please save me from all of my nonsense. Let me be perfect in my understanding, perfect in my practice, perfect in my words, perfect in my thoughts, perfect in my actions, in all times, places and circumstances. In that mood chant your japa and the miracles will happen. With every syllable, you will be moving forward, back to your original, pure identity as a pure devotee of the Lord.

Damayanti devi dasi: How come the great personalities like lord Brahma are in fear of the Supreme Personality of Godhead?

SDA: That means, they are acting under His direction. They have to obey Him. That's what it means.

Hare Krishna Das: Advanced devotees are constantly engaged in service, neophyte devotees do service and take some relaxation before the next service. Why this phenomenon and how one can be 24 hours engaged in service?

SDA: We are allowed to take some rest. At night we take some rest. Prabhupada even said, if you are sleepy, take a nap. Not too much but just to get refreshed. We are allowed to take some rest. We have material bodies and they have some limits. We are allowed to take some relaxation. But we should not overdo it. That's all. It should be balanced. Ok.

Bahurupa Caitanya Das: How to subdue the mind? It is always disturbed in its whim. I have proven to be a failure to do so, it has become my enemy, how to pass this test, please help me.

SDA: I would recommend memorize this verse (BG 6.26):

yato yato niścalati
manaś cañcalam asthiram
tatas tato niyamyaitad
ātmany eva vaśaṁ nayet

"From wherever the mind wanders due to its flickering and unsteady nature, one must certainly withdraw it and bring it back under the control of the Self."

I would memorize that verse and chant it often. That's what I suggest. Krishna's specific instruction about controlling the mind. Memorize the verse in Sanskrit and in your local language if you speak Spanish. Memorize it in English and Spanish and recite it often throughout the day. Whenever you see your mind is going off the track, do it again. yato yato niscalati...

Amala Purana: If the government puts an abrupt end to activities like slaughterhouse and liquor shops, then the general populace will revolt and bring down the government. So how Vaisnava government can drive away Kali, practically in this present age?

SDA: You have to educate the people, that's why massive book distribution is very important. We have to educate everybody in these days of democracy. Not that we have a powerful king who forces citizens to do whatever he wants. Now it's the days of democracy. If they don't like the government leader, they get rid of him and bring someone else. We have to educate the people in general. You want to close the slaughterhouse; we have to convince the people that they don't want slaughterhouse anymore. We have to convince them not to buy the products of slaughterhouse and liquor shops. That's the best way in the present situation. Convince people not to buy meat anymore, not to buy liquor anymore, don't go to the brothels anymore. Convince them not to do these things.

Bhadra devi dasi: How to effectively pray to Krishna to make me a pure devotee? When will I recognize that I am responsible for the precarious position..

SDA: *Hare Krishna Hare Krishna Krishna Krishna Hare Hare, Hare Rama Hare Rama Rama Rama Hare Hare.* That's the most powerful prayer, Bhadra Devi dasi, for becoming a pure devotee.

You are responsible, you are in Maya right now Bhadra Devi. It's your fault that you are caught up in the cycle of birth and death. That's why you have to beg Krishna, "Please get me out of here my dear Lord, please get me back to my original position in Your pure loving service, please take me."

Devotee: How can Lord Siva be in charge of ignorance, if he is one of the greatest Vaishnava?

SDA: That's the duty he has been given. Whatever duty is given to pure devotes, they accept it.

Just like here for example, in the modern-day government, some very highly qualified person is put in charge of the prison. Does it mean he is a criminal? No. A very highly qualified government servant, very loyal, law-abiding government servant is made in charge of the prison.

VPM (Vishnu Priya Mataji): He can handle those in mode of ignorance, all the hobgoblins and all.

SDA: He is powerful enough to keep them under his control. That's another reason. Gurumataji (**VPM**) is making that point.

Bhakta Ravi Kolluru: When our goal is to make the whole world Krishna conscious, how can we be compassionate to those who cannot follow the regulative principles, even if they aspire for it?

SDA: We have to be compassionate. Compassion is the key. Not that by hating people you can make them Krishna conscious. It's by the compassion of other devotees that I became a devotee, compassion of Vishnujana Swami. Compassion is how we are successful in making people Krishna conscious, you can't force them. It's by compassion, kindness, and love because in material world there is no genuine compassion; everyone is exploiting. They talk about love, but its all facade. There is no genuine love and compassion in the material world. It's cheating business, they are just trying to be the enjoyer, that's all. Genuine compassion is only there from the pure devotees and that compassion is what inspires one to follow the regulative principles.

Nandini: Is it true that if one has genuine love for Lord Siva, that it would inspire them to become Krishna's devotee?

SDA: Lord Siva is a pure devotee. If you have some motive in approaching Lord Siva then you will become one of his hobgoblins. If you are approaching him with genuine love, he is a great Vaishnava. He will inspire you to become like he is, a great devotee of Krishna.

Bahurupa Caitanya: How to become Krishna conscious when a person is in mode of ignorance effectively?

SDA: Those of us who are in mode of ignorance, how can we get out of Maya? We want to sleep all day long. Whenever we get disturbed, we just sleep, sleep, sleep, that's what they do. When our mind gets disturbed, we go to sleep. How do you get out of that mode of ignorance? One thing is don't overeat. If you overeat, that can put you to sleep. Regulate your eating. Don't overeat. Eat balanced amount of prasadam that can help. Don't eat too much. Don't eat too many sweets. Don't overdo your senses. When you do that, you will go into mode of ignorance very easily. By regulating your senses, you can conquer the mode of ignorance.

Devotee: Should I do personal endeavor to please Shiva?

SDA: No, you should focus on being a devotee of Krishna. Not that you become a devotee of Shiva. No. Shiva wants us to be a devotee of Krishna, so go ahead and do what pleases him the most. Shiva is most pleased when you come to Krishna. That's what you should do. If you want to please Shiva, you have to become Krishna's pure devotee. That will please Shiva.

Hare Krishna Das: What is the proper consciousness for chanting Hare Krishna?

SDA: You are begging for pure devotional service. Not that you are begging Krishna, "Krishna give me this,

Krishna give me that". You are begging Krishna "Please make me Your pure devotee. Please free me from all my nonsense and let me be Your pure devotee, please my Lord. Let my every thought, word, deed in all times, places and circumstances be completely pleasing to You." That's the mood for chanting Hare Krishna.

Caitanya Das: The amount of impurities I have is giving me hopelessness. But I do want to become pure in this lifetime; however with these impurities, how will I ever be able to offer my heart to Krishna? How will I get pure?

SDA: That's the mood. Save me a fallen, Your Divine Grace. The more you feel you are a hopeless basket case, "There is no hope of ever becoming Krishna conscious". The more you feel hopeless and totally dependent on Krishna's mercy, that's when you actually become liberated. Just like our acaryas, they say, "I have no taste." Even Lord Caitanya prayed, "I have no attraction for the Holy names." Lord Caitanya prayed He had no attraction for the Holy Names because that's our position. He said, "Unfortunate as I am, I have no attraction." Lord Caitanya Himself prayed. Actually He is stating our position. That is our position. We have no attraction for Hare Krishna. We just want to eat, sleep, mate and defend. But by the mercy of Lord Caitanya Mahaprabhu, by the mercy of Srila Prabhupada, by the mercy of the Spiritual Master, the Vaishnavas… the more you feel hopeless, that's when the mercy actually comes. The more you feel desperate and hopeless, that's when mercy flows like anything to save you. It's very good, if you feel hopeless. Keep that mercy of hopelessness. That's how you will attract the mercy Caitanya Das.

Hare Krishna Hare Krishna Krishna Krishna Hare Hare,
Hare Rama Hare Rama Rama Rama Hare Hare.

Srila Prabhupada ki jaya!

Why remain in a suffering condition when all you have to do is tune in and turn on your soul? I wrote a song to introduce this concept to the music listeners of the world:

Turn On Your Soul

Do you know who you really are?

Do you know where you're coming from?

Do you know for sure where you're going?

Or what you will become?

You're eternal, full of knowledge and bliss

So remember and celebrate this.

You're not of this world, dear friend.

Better tune in and turn on your soul.

Do you know what happens when you die?

Do you know what's beyond the sky?

Do you think that body is you?

It's just something that you're passing through.

You're eternal, full of knowledge and bliss

So remember and celebrate this.

You're not of this world, dear friend.

Better tune in and turn on your soul.

We're told that everything happens by chance.

That the universe has no person in control.

But I see that every machine has got an operator.

So the universe also has one.

This I know.

Do you know who you really are?

Do you know where you're coming from?

Do you know for sure where you're going?

Or what you will become?

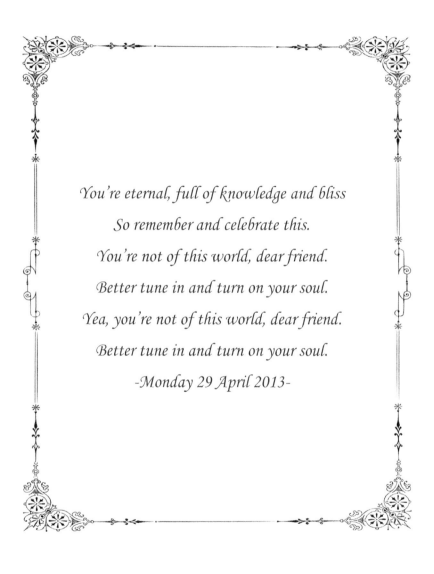

You're eternal, full of knowledge and bliss

So remember and celebrate this.

You're not of this world, dear friend.

Better tune in and turn on your soul.

Yea, you're not of this world, dear friend.

Better tune in and turn on your soul.

-Monday 29 April 2013-

Lesson 2

ECSTASY OF PURE DEVOTIONAL SERVICE

~~~ ~~~ ~~~

Srimad Bhagavatam 3.29.13

Austin, Texas

Date: 20-JAN-2021

Om Namo Bhagavate Vasudevaya

[Gurudeva sings three times and devotees repeat]

sālokya-sārṣṭi-sāmīpya-
sārūpyaikatvam apy uta
dīyamānaṁ na gṛhṇanti
vinā mat-sevanaṁ janāḥ

Synonyms

sālokya — living on the same planet; *sārṣṭi* — having the same opulence; *sāmīpya* — to be a personal associate; *sārūpya* — having the same bodily features; *ekatvam* — oneness; *api* — also; *uta* — even; *dīyamānam* — being offered; *na* — not; *gṛhṇanti* — do accept; *vinā* — without; *mat* — My; *sevanam* — devotional service; *janāḥ* — pure devotees.

Translation

"A pure devotee does not accept any kind of liberation — salokya, sarsti, samipya, sarupya or ekatva — even though they are offered by the Supreme Personality of Godhead."

Purport

Lord Caitanya teaches us how to execute pure devotional service out of spontaneous love for the Supreme Personality of Godhead. In the *Siksastaka,* He prays to the Lord: "O Lord, I do not wish to gain from You any wealth, nor do I wish to have a beautiful wife, nor do I wish to have many followers. All I want from You is that in life after life I may remain a pure devotee at Your lotus feet." There is a similarity between the prayers of Lord Caitanya and the statements of *Srimad-Bhagavatam.* Lord Caitanya prays, "in life after life," indicating that a devotee does not even desire the cessation of birth and death. The *yogis* and empiric philosophers desire cessation of the process of birth and death, but a devotee is satisfied even to remain in this material world and execute devotional service.

It is clearly stated herein that a pure devotee does not desire *ekatva,* oneness with the Supreme Lord, as desired by the impersonalists, the mental speculators and the meditators. To become one with the Supreme Lord is beyond the dream of a pure devotee. Sometimes he may accept promotion to the Vaikuntha planets to serve the Lord there, but he will never accept merging into the Brahman effulgence, which he considers worse than hellish. Such *ekatva,* or merging into the effulgence of the Supreme Lord, is called *kaivalya,* but the happiness derived from *kaivalya* is considered by the pure devotee to be hellish. The devotee is so fond of rendering service to the Supreme Lord that the five kinds of liberation are not important to him. If one is engaged in pure transcendental loving service to the Lord, it is understood that he has already achieved the five kinds of liberation.

When a devotee is promoted to the spiritual world, Vaikuntha, he receives four kinds of facilities. One of these is *salokya,* living on the same planet as the Supreme Personality. The Supreme Person, in His different plenary expansions, lives on innumerable Vaikuntha planets, and the chief planet is Krsnaloka. Just as within the material universe the chief planet is the sun, in the spiritual world the chief planet is Krsnaloka. From Krsnaloka, the bodily effulgence of Lord Krsna is distributed not only to the spiritual world but to the material world as well; it is covered by matter, however, in the material world. In the spiritual world there are innumerable Vaikuntha planets, and on each one the Lord is the predominating Deity. A devotee can be promoted to one such Vaikuntha planet to live with the Supreme Personality of Godhead.

In *sarsti* liberation the opulence of the devotee is equal to the opulence of the Supreme Lord. *Samipya* means to be a personal associate of the Supreme Lord. In *sarupya* liberation the bodily features of the devotee are exactly like those of the Supreme Person but for two or three symptoms found exclusively on the transcendental body of the Lord. Srivatsa, for example, the hair on the chest of the Lord, particularly distinguishes Him from His devotees.

A pure devotee does not accept these five kinds of spiritual existence, even if they are offered, and he certainly does not hanker after material benefits, which are all insignificant in comparison with spiritual benefits. When Prahlada Maharaja was offered some material benefit, he stated, "My Lord, I have seen that my father achieved all kinds of material benefits, and even the demigods were afraid of his opulence, but still, in a second, You have finished his life and all his material prosperity." For a devotee there is no question of desiring any material or spiritual prosperity. He simply aspires to serve the Lord. That is his highest happiness. (End of Purport)

Sankarshan das Adhikari (SDA): This is a very amazing verse. A pure devotee does not desire any kind of liberation-*salokya, sashtir,samipya, sarupya or ekatva* – even though they are offered by the Supreme Personality of Godhead.

Ekatva – the impersonal Brahman realization. So just see how satisfying the pure devotional service is. Of course, a devotee is taken back to home back to godhead. And we are thinking "I would like to go back to home back to godhead", but actually a pure devotee doesn't even think "I need to go back to home back to Godhead". That's called salokya liberation. You live on the same planet with the Lord, either on the Krishna loka planet or one of the Vaikuntha planets. A pure devotee does not even desire that, because he is already fully connected with the

Lord, right here, right now on this planet, doesn't matter where he is. He can be in the spiritual world or the material world, doesn't matter where the pure devotee is, because he is intimately connected in pure loving relationship with Krishna at every minute.

Lord Chaitanya said, "let me take birth, life after life". A pure devotee does not think "I have to get out of this cycle of birth and death". He thinks "I don't mind remaining in the cycle of birth and death as long as I am engaged in pure devotional service." That's all. The ecstasy in pure devotional service surpasses all these kinds of liberation.

The ecstasy of pure devotional service is so amazing that even if you are in an extremely painful condition of this material existence, you will experience a sweet ecstasy. There is a nice example in this connection. During the battlefield of Kurukshetra, Krishna was a charioteer and Arjuna was the fighter. In other words, Krishna didn't act as a fighter, He simply acted as a charioteer. He drove the chariot for Arjuna. That's all He did.

Now in the battlefield, there are rules in Ksatriya culture, you don't shoot arrows at the chariot driver; you don't kill the chariot driver. You only go for the warrior himself. The chariot drivers are immune from the battlefield. In the modern-day warfare, it does not matter whether you are a fighter, or you are driving a tank, in either way they want to kill you no matter who you are. Because you are on battlefield, they want to kill everyone. Even if you are just driving a jeep, they want to kill you. But in actual Ksatriya system, the chariot driver is never killed. But in this particular case, the son of Dronacharya Ashwathama, he came after Krishna against the rules to shoot Him with the arrows. Now Arjuna could not tolerate this, being a devotee of Krishna. "I am not going to allow my beloved Lord to be shot with all these arrows." Actually, it was like a shower, a huge barrage of arrows, like a machine gun, (sound effect) were coming at Krishna's body. What did Arjuna do? He stood as a human shield and he is accepting all these arrows shooting his body. Showers of arrows penetrating his body. But he took every single arrow and Krishna was not hit by one arrow. But the amazing thing is that instead of feeling that horrible painful condition, Arjuna is experiencing the sweetest nectar. The shower of arrows penetrating his body, he was experiencing the sweetest nectar. The point is this, if one is actually engaged in pure devotional service, there is nothing in this material world that can make one miserable or unhappy. Even the most distressful thing, even being shot by volumes of arrows or bullets or whatever, it's just the sweetest nectar.

The difficulty is that we are not in pure devotional service. Even if we step our toe, we start screaming in pain feeling very unhappy – "O, I hurt my toe, or cut my finger, or I bump my elbow, we get all disturbed." Just consider how much we are still on the bodily plane. How much we are still on the platform of trying to enjoy this material world. This is the difficulty. We are still trying to enjoy this material world. This is a great, great difficulty. We are not convinced that this material world is simply a place of misery. We are still thinking that there must be some happiness here. Here we are in a desert dying of thirst, and we are thinking that if somebody brings a drop of water and we think 'aaaaah' great relief. We stick out our tongue and drink that drop of water. "Oh, that is so wonderful." Can a drop of water satisfy you in a desert? Absolutely not! We are taking the cheap thrills of material sense gratification as actual satisfaction of the self. These cheap thrills don't satisfy us at all. It is time for us to become enlightened.

teṣāṁ satata-yuktānāṁ
bhajatāṁ prīti-pūrvakam
dadāmi buddhi-yogaṁ taṁ
yena mām upayānti te

(BG 10.10)

It's time for us to come to the platform of devotional service and become liberated from all these difficulties, all these tortures of the material existence. Devotees can go through exactly the same thing that the non- devotees are going through – birth, death, old age, disease, poverty, wealth, sickness, and health. These dualities are constantly bouncing us up and down on the ocean of material existence, waves are bumping us up and down, up and down. But the devotee becomes transcendentally situated beyond these dualities. **BG 2.14**:

mātrā-sparśās tu kaunteya
śītoṣṇa-sukha-duḥkha-dāḥ
āgamāpāyino 'nityās
tāṁs titikṣasva bhārata

"The non-permanent appearance of happiness and distress, and their disappearance in due course, are like the appearance and disappearance of winter and summer seasons. They arise from sense perception, O scion of Bharata, and one must learn to tolerate them without being disturbed."

The way to become tolerant just like Arjuna. Why was Arjuna not devasted by that shower of arrows penetrating his skin? Why did it not bother him? Because he was fully absorbed in the loving service to Krishna. He could only think that, I have to protect my beloved Krishna. If we always keep serving Krishna, pleasing Krishna, loving Krishna and loving and serving guru, loving guru, pleasing guru, we always keep these in forefront of our consciousness 24/7 *desh kal patra* – in all times, places and circumstances, we will never feel the pinch of material nature ever again.

But now we are being pinched, pinched, pinched, pinched, and pinched and screaming in agony because we are not in the mood of pleasing Krishna. We are thinking "how can I become happy." "How can I become pleased". Of course, the intelligent person understands, "Okay, I want to be happy, how do I do it". There is nothing wrong with the desire to be happy, but you just have to go the right way. You have to go by the right way. The hand wants nourishment, it is not wrong for the hand to want nourishment. It needs nourishment. But the hand has to be intelligent to know, "I don't get nourished by squeezing the food in my fingers." I get my nourishment by putting the food to the mouth, and then it goes to the belly. There is nothing wrong with the desire to be happy. It is a natural desire to want to be happy because that is your actual nature. But one has to be intelligent to know what the actual means to become happy. If you try to become happy artificially as the materialist do, then you will never really be happy. You may think that you are happy sometimes, it's called 'maya-sukhaya', or illusory happiness.

Qualification to see Krishna

There is no happiness in this material existence, only the mirage or illusion of happiness. We have to become very very eager to experience Krishna, to see Krishna. Even Prabhupada told me in one letter that "Now you must become qualified to see Krishna face to face." Instead of trying to be the enjoyer of this material world, we should try to qualify ourselves to see Krishna face to face. That's the result of pure devotional service. Seeing Krishna face to face means that I become a pure devotee.

Prabhupada says we should become very very eager to see Krishna. He gives the example of one thief. He was hearing a Bhagavat reciter. explaining how Krishna is wandering in the forest, a little baby Krishna is wandering in the forest, loaded with all kinds of valuable jewels. And this thief was thinking, "Really, a little boy up in the Vrindavan loaded with valuable jewels, wandering all alone in the forest with no parental supervision. Aah, yes, I will go to Vrindavan, and I will find that boy. I will take those jewels and become a millionaire overnight." In this way, the thief became very enthused to go to Vrindavan. So, he is going to Vrindavan, all the way from South India to Vrindavan. They didn't have the bus or the planes or the trains in those days, just walking, maybe an oxcart. But he was walking & walking for many many days and many many weeks. Walking across India, from south India to Vrindavan he was thinking that I will go to Vrindavan and find that boy and I'll become very wealthy. I'll take those jewels. After many many days and weeks, he finally arrives in Vrindavan. And he goes into the forest in the night and he is looking where is that boy! Where is that boy? Normally no one is qualified to see Krishna except for the pure devotees but sometimes even the materialists become very very very eager to see Krishna and Krishna reveals Himself. Just see Krishna is so kind, even by intense eagerness even for a materialist Krishna can sometimes reveal himself, what to speak of a devotee. So he was saying, "Where is that boy? where is that boy? Where is that boy? Where is that boy? And one night there He was, Krishna." He said "O Krishna! You have so many valuable jewels. You are a nice boy" He tried to flatter him. "You are so nice, boy. You have so many valuable jewels, can you give me some?" Thinking that by flattering the boy he can win Him. Just like You give a kid a piece of candy or something to flatter him. I'll give you whatever you want. Krishna says," No, no, no, no! My mother, Yasoda, she will scold me!" The pet son of mother Yashoda. (chuckles). That thief, even though he had all material desires to steal the jewels from that boy Krishna but just by having that darshan of Krishna, he became a pure devotee. He became a pure devotee with that darshan! Then Krishna said, "alright you can take it."

Just see! We should become very, very eager to become qualified to see Krishna. Become very, very eager to see

Krishna and that qualification is not going to Vrindavan to steal the jewels. That qualification is pure devotional service. Of course, we must become very, very eager that I must become a pure devotee.

I must become a pure devotee! So I can see my beloved Lord. That intensity of desire and Prabhupada says, how do you get that? You get that from the association of devotees. Like in the material world, they are very eager. "I must become a millionaire, I must become a rockstar, I must become the president of the United States of America," they have this enthusiasm, this eagerness for this thing or that thing. We should take that same tendency and apply it to Krishna consciousness. That's the point. In this way, everybody wants to get ahead right. The ultimate getting ahead is becoming a pure devotee of Krishna. So, everyone should hanker, hanker, hanker that I must become a pure devotee. I must become a pure devotee! I must become a pure devotee. That eagerness should be there in the heart of everyone. We need to find those devotees who are very enthusiastic to be pure devotees. Take shelter of them, take guidance from them, and follow their instructions. Take advantage of their example. In our movement, we have some devotees who are very eager to be pure devotees of Krishna. We should take their association, we should learn from them, hear from them, and we should serve them. In this way, by associating with those devotees who are very eager for pure bhakti, we will also get that eagerness for pure bhakti. That eagerness for pure devotional service is recommended by Rupa Goswami.

utsahan niscayad dhairyat
tat-tat-karma-pravartanat

Question & answers:

Devotee: If we see that someone is offending a devotee, what should be done at that moment?

SDA: It could be dangerous, but we should try to convince them not to do that if that is possible. Find some way to stop to do it from doing that. If not possible, better to leave. If someone is offending a devotee, you should try to stop him from doing that.

VPM: Depending on time, place, and circumstances.

SDA: Gurumataji is saying depending on the situation. But if it is possible to put a stop to it you should do it. "Prabhu, Prabhu what are you doing? Calm down!". It depends on the situation. Look at what Arjuna did. His mood, if someone is coming to offend Krishna, he took the arrows on himself. That was his mood for protecting Krishna from being offended by Aswathama. "Let me take the arrows." In the same mood of Arjuna wanting to protect Krishna from being offended, as far as possible we should always protect the devotees from being offended. That's Vaishnav seva.

Amala Purana: Your grace mentioned we need to be intensely eager to become pure devotees of the Lord, so what to do if someone has very little eagerness? Some eagerness but not so much. How to develop an intense desire to become a pure devotee?

SDA: You are realizing that you should have it, that's good. Then you pray for it "my dear Lord please bless me, please bless me with the eagerness to become your pure devotee!" and you can chant Hare Krishna in that mood, begging for pure devotion.

Sarva dharman parityajya

Mam ekam sharanamvraja

Yes, Krishna is ordering you to fully surrender right now.

Why are you not following Krishna? Why are you remaining on the mental platform? You know it's like a bunch of people swimming in the water and having a great time and saying "Come on in the water, it's fun."

"I don't know" you stand, dip your toes in. I don't know it's a little chilly to me.

VPM: Everything is given. What is the difficulty? Your only difficulty is that we don't take it.

SDA: Yes! Isn't it? Why are you making it difficult, that is called the mental platform. Just jump in and dive in and just do it. That's all. Why are you holding back?

Chakravarti: Happiness we feel is false in the material world as you explained, what is the symptom of the soul being happy?

SDA: The symptom is spiritual happiness; it is uninterrupted by any material circumstance. It's steady in every single situation. Spiritual happiness means in all situations happiness and distress, heat and cold, honour and dishonour, poverty and wealth.

VPM: no hankering and no lamentation

SDA: in all situations.

SDA: no hankering no lamentation and always feel how Krishna is showering unlimited blessing upon you at every minute. That's spiritual happiness. In every situation, even at the moment of death, there's no unhappiness.

na socati na kanksati

VPM: Yes, so when you are thinking about something, and we don't get it then we are miserable. But pure devotee doesn't have any....

SDA: Pure devotee's only desire is pure devotional service pleasing Krishna. One can please Krishna in any situation. The pure devotee's only desire is to please his beloved Krishna. In every situation, you simply have to have the proper attitude to devotional service. You might be a highly qualified expert in this thing and that thing, but you are not required to be an expert in this thing and that thing. Just the attitude of devotional service is all you require. It is sometimes said that it is the attitude, not the aptitude that determines your altitude. Even if you are not very good at doing anything, if you have the right attitude, you'll be in a state of bliss. Just keep that right attitude. "I want to serve Krishna, I want to learn from the devotees, I want to learn from the spiritual master, I want to learn from the scriptures, I want to learn how to perfect my service more and more and more every day. If you have that mood of always trying to move forward in Krishna consciousness, always trying to please Guru, always trying to please Vaishnavas, always trying to please Krishna, then the pinching of the material nature will no longer disturb you.

VPM: the pinching of material nature will be there.

SDA: It would be there but they won't disturb you. You will still get sick, old, and die.

Caryn Milburn: What is the difference between begging to be a pure devotee and praying for spiritual things? Which is not acceptable?

SDA: The habit we have in this material world is – God give me that, give me this, give me, give me, give me. I need this, I need a raise, I need a new house, I need a new car, I need a new spouse, (chuckles) whatever. They are praying for material things. Our spiritual prayer is- *Hare Krishna, Hare Krishna, Krishna Krishna, Hare Hare/ Hare Rama, Hare Rama, Rama Rama Hare Hare. Hare* refers to Radharani actually. My dear mother Radharani and my dear Krishna, please bless me with pure devotional service. That's the prayer, that's our spiritual prayer. That's the spiritual thing we are praying for. Begging to be a pure devotee and begging for pure devotional service is the same thing. "Krishna please make me Your pure devotee," and "Krishna please engage me in pure devotional service" is the same thing. No difference.

Paramahamsa das: By getting inspired by sincere devotees, but we are not able to apply it right away. Is there any hope in the future of being inspired throughout my life?

SDA: Sure

Paramhamsa das: Is there any hope for me?

SDA: Let's put it this way. You have to try your best to apply it right now. Trust no future, however pleasant. "I am very inspired by this instruction; I might try it next week". "I am really inspired by the idea- no gambling, no illicit sex, no intoxication, and no meat-eating and chanting 16 rounds. That looks like a pretty good deal. I become qualified to see God face to face. That's pretty good. I think I will do it sometime later maybe next week, next year, or maybe I want to get graduate from college after I retire" Don't postpone it. You embrace it immediately. What is that saying, if something is auspicious, do it immediately and if something is inauspicious, postpone it. It was advised in that way.

VPM: Kalidas, in Ramayana.

SDA: In the Ramayana, if something is auspicious, do it immediately, and if something is inauspicious postpone it. If you are inspired to be a pure devotee, apply it immediately. If you postpone it, you will lose your inspiration.

VPM: not losing it but …..

SDA: if you don't apply it, you will lose it, you will lose the inspiration.

VPM: you lose your chance also.

SDA: Yes.

VPM: Because that can be at any time, any moment.

Paramatma dasa: In the purport, it says that 'samipya' means to be a personal associate of the Lord, does it mean salokya and sashtir, will they not get the personal association of the Lord?

SDA: Salokya living on the same planet as the Lord, it is possible not to have so much direct association with the Lord even when on the same planet.

The Pure devotee is transcendental to all these things. Because he is already associating with the lord at every minute because he has embraced the Lord's orders as his very life and soul. He has fully

embraced Krishna's orders as his very life and soul, therefore he is constantly associating with Krishna at every minute. In spite of not going back to Godhead to be with Krishna, he is already with Krishna even here in this material existence.

Bhakta Jitu: How much time will it take to clean the dirty things from the heart if one sincerely begs for devotional service?

SDA: It can be done in one second or it can take millions of lifetimes. Bhakta Jitu it depends on your determination and your enthusiasm. It can be done within a nanosecond or it can take millions and millions of lifetimes.

It really depends on your intensity of your sincerity, the intensity of your enthusiasm. You can immediately become a pure devotee instantly (**BS 5**).

premanjana-cchurita-bhakti-vilocanena
santah sadaiva hrdayesu vilokayanti

yam syamasundaram acintya-guna-svarupam
govindam adi-purusam tam aham bhajami

"I worship Govinda primeval Lord, Shyamsundar, Krishna himself with inconceivable, innumerable attributes which the pure devotees see in their heart of hearts with the eye of devotion tinged with the salve of love".

So, they don't need to go back to Godhead to achieve that. They experience that, they see Krishna within their hearts because their eyes are tinged with the salve of love. You just have to learn how to get that ointment of love for Godhead, in Sanskrit it is called *premanjana*, the ointment of love of God. We simply have to anoint our eyes with the ointment of the love of God. Where do you get that *premanjana*? That comes from the pure devotees. Pure devotes has that *premanjana*. Our Srila Prabhupada has that *premanjana*. If you follow Prabhupada's instructions very seriously then Prabhupada will bless you with this *premanjana*, your eyes will always become anointed with the love of God then you will see Krishna directly within your heart. Directly you will see Krishna face to face, eye to eye. Then you can manifest externally also. Prabhupada said – "hankering internally, you constantly see Me in front of you standing there with His three-fold bending form, playing the flute with the peacock feather in His hair". We see externally also, standing in front of you. These things can all be achieved by awakening pure love of Godhead within the heart.

Srila Prabhupada ki Jai!

Granthraj Srimad Bhagwatam ki Jai !

Gaur Premanande! HARIBOL!

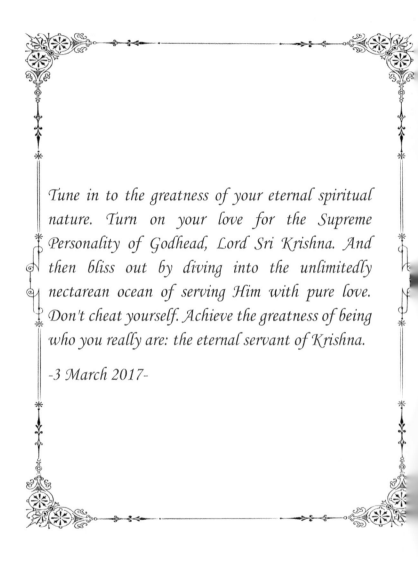

Tune in to the greatness of your eternal spiritual nature. Turn on your love for the Supreme Personality of Godhead, Lord Sri Krishna. And then bliss out by diving into the unlimitedly nectarean ocean of serving Him with pure love. Don't cheat yourself. Achieve the greatness of being who you really are: the eternal servant of Krishna.

-3 March 2017-

Lesson 3

NEVER BE CARRIED AWAY BY ATHEISTIC PROPAGANDA

∾∾ ∾∾ ∾∾

Srimad Bhagavatam 3.29.40

Austin, Texas

Date: 17-FEB-2021

Om Namo Bhagavate Vasudevaya

[Gurudeva sings three times and devotees repeat]

*yad-bhayād
vāti vāto 'yaṁ
sūryas tapati yad-bhayāt
yad-bhayād varṣate devo
bha-gaṇo bhāti yad-bhayāt*

Synonyms

yat — of whom (the Supreme Personality of Godhead); *bhayāt* — out of fear; *vāti* — blows; *vātaḥ* — the wind; *ayam* — this; *sūryaḥ* — sun; *tapati* — shines; *yat* — of whom; *bhayāt* — out of fear; *yat* — of whom; *bhayāt* — out of fear; *varṣate* — sends rains; *devaḥ* — the god of rain; *bha-gaṇaḥ* — the host of heavenly bodies; *bhāti* — shine; *yat* — of whom; *bhayāt* — out of fear.

Translation

Out of fear of the Supreme Personality of Godhead the wind blows, out of fear of Him the sun shines, out of fear of Him the rain pours forth showers, and out of fear of Him the host of heavenly bodies shed their luster.

Purport

The Lord states in _Bhagavad-gītā, mayādhyakṣeṇa prakṛtiḥ sūyate:_ "Nature is working under My direction." The foolish person thinks that nature is working automatically, but such an atheistic theory is not supported in the Vedic literature. Nature is working under the superintendence of the Supreme Personality of Godhead. That is confirmed in _Bhagavad-gītā,_ and we also find here that the sun shines under the direction of the Lord, and the cloud pours forth showers of rain under the direction of the Lord. All natural phenomena are under superintendence of the Supreme Personality of Godhead, Viṣṇu. [End of purport]

Sankarshan Das Adhikari:

So, the atheists think that nature is working automatically. In the beginning, there was nothing, and that nothing exploded, and out of that explosion of nothing came this amazingly, intricately designed universe. But I ask you is that logical? Even if there was something in the beginning – some lump and you exploded it, since when have we seen that an explosion causes something of order? Just like this nice house here at 10,700 Johnwood way. If we took a bunch of bricks and what they call sidewall and all kinds of building material bags of cement, wires, and all kinds of raw ingredients and stuck it in a stack and put a stick of dynamite in there. Room! We got this house of that, would you believe that? Can you create an order by the explosion? That is the point. No, explosions break down to order. The atheists say there was a big bang and this whole beautiful universe came out of that explosion. That is one absurdity, and the other thing is, they say, it all came out of nothing. The fact is nothing comes out of nothing. So, if you want to consider this theistic philosophy, the logic behind the atheistic philosophy you will see that this theistic philosophy is logical. Creations are made by creators. Just like a beautiful painting doesn't just pop out of nowhere. An artist makes it. Just like an automobile popped out of nothing. No. Some engineer designed the whole thing. So, we see that creations don't pop out of nothing, they come from creators. There was an original creator, that is a logical step. To say that there was no original creator, it just came out of nothing, is blind faith dogma. No. It is actual science and logic to understand that, there is a supreme original creator behind everything. Some say, why do you say it is male, why can't we have a female source of all existence? Just you men are chauvinists, so you say it is a He, the original person is a He. Well actually, if you look at nature when a child is born, who gives the seed? Does the mother give the seed or does the father gives the seed? The original source of the living entity is the father. He plants the seed. Of course, the mother is more affectionate that is also there. There is nothing like the affection of the mother. All the trouble she goes through for the child, nursing the child, bearing the child in her womb, in terms of affection the mother is always the winner. She is more affectionate than the father. But the father is the original source. So, the original source of all existence, therefore, is a person. We should not be carried away by the atheistic propaganda of the rascal atheists the *asuric bhava*, who take up the atheistic nature of the demon. They want to establish themselves as the Supreme. They want to deny any other supremacy other than their own. So, we should not become misled by the atheistic propaganda mongers, who are giving us all these false dogmas, all these false philosophies simply to justify sense gratification.

Where does sense gratification take you?

What does the Bible say? The wages of sin is death. So, sense gratification will simply lead you to death. That is all. It kills you, it is death. Every time you engage in sense gratification; you are calling death. Come now and get me, I am here. Death, now I am ready. Come and take me, take me. The devotees are intelligent. They don't engage in material sense gratification. "*Hrisikena Hrisikesha sevanam*". They engage their senses in the service of the master of the senses. That brings them beyond death. They come to deathlessness. Even Prabhupada explains in one lecture. "Deathlessness begins from the moment of initiation". That is when you actually enter into your eternal identity. We practically, formally enter into, when you take initiation. But not some superficial initiation. You sit for initiation and do whatever you want. No. When you actually take initiation seriously, that now I have become initiated by the bonafide spiritual master and now I am duty bound to carry out his orders in all places, in all times and in all circumstances. I must be fully obedient to the bonafide spiritual master. When you take initiation seriously for what actually it is not and not some show-bottle thing but actually for what it is, that is when you become a liberated soul, that is when you become deathless. You achieve immortality from the very day of initiation. You stick to your vows. But if you give up your vows then you go back into the world of mortality. You have given up your position of immortality and gone back to mortality. So, those who prefer mortality they can have it. But those who are intelligent, realize that mortality in this material world as Bhaktisiddhanta Saraswati says, "This material world is not a fit place for a gentleman's living". This is a realm of rogues and rascals. It is not a very nice place. There is so much cheating that is going in, just like what happened in Washington DC. The outgoing President couldn't accept that he was losing, so he wanted to block the counting of the votes for the new President by sending mobs to attack the Capitol building. This is the kind of so-called government leaders we have nowadays.

Actually, Prabhupada told us that we should be the leaders of the world. That is the actual position. Acharya means one who is an ideal leader.

> *yad yad ācarati śreṣṭhas*
> *tat tad evetaro janaḥ*
> *sa yat pramāṇaṁ kurute*
> *lokas tad anuvartate*

(BG 3.21)

"Whatever action a great man performs, common men follow in his footsteps. Whatever standard he sets by exemplary acts the whole world pursues".

So, ISKCON is meant to create acharyas. Here we are struggling neophytes still engaged in sense gratification, over-eating, over-sleeping, finding fault, fighting with each other, and breaking the regulative principles. It is time for us to get serious now about what Prabhupada wants us to be. He wants us to become acharyas by whose example and by whose teachings the whole world can come to its original position of devotion to the Supreme Personality of Godhead. Of course, it has been deteriorating. In Satya yuga, the age of less crime, the whole place was pious and everyone was a devotee. In the Treta yuga, it went down to 75% pious and 25% demoniac. In the Dwapara yuga, it went down to 50-50. In the Kali yuga, it is 75% impious and 25% pious. It is going down 25, 24, 23, 22, and when it goes down to point of zero, then the Kalki avatar will come and annihilate all the rascals to bring in another Satya Yuga. So, we are meant to be the agents of the Supreme Personality of Godhead. We are meant to be agents of Lord Chaitanya Mahaprabhu to bring about a spiritual revolution. It is actually predicted. In the Puranas, there is a statement that there is a 10,000-year period where the whole world will be filled up with devotees. So, we are meant now to be the agents of fulfilling that prediction. The ten thousand years period started in 1486, a little over 500 years ago. It began in 1486. The Chaitanya era, is a 10,000-year period in which the whole world will become Krishna conscious. ISKCON now is bringing it forward, Srila Prabhupada is bringing it forward and we are meant to be the agents of Srila Prabhupada by totally surrendering ourselves and following the instructions of Srila Prabhupada. Prabhupada will empower us to act as his agents for bringing the full-blown Chaitanya era on this planet as soon as possible. The devotees can't tolerate to see the suffering of the living entities. This is too much. They can't tolerate to see all these cows going to the slaughter houses and all these babies going to the abortion clinics and being murdered. The devotees can't tolerate this. Therefore, they want to preach, they want to give out all these books. They want to awaken people to Krishna consciousness so that this world can become a fit place for a gentleman's living, instead of just a *bhoga loka* (a place of sense enjoyment).

This Krishna conscious movement is most sublime and here we read today that out of fear of the Supreme Lord, the wind blows, the sun shines, the rain pours, showers everything is going on under the direction of the Lord. So, you may wonder why under the direction of the Lord, all hell is breaking loose on this planet right now. They say it is all God's fault. Because He is the Supreme controller, it is all His fault. But no, He gives us freedom also. Because He wants our love. Love means voluntary. So, Krishna wants our love, He does not want puppets. Because He wants the devotees who voluntarily choose to love Him, since that voluntary choice is there, there is always an option that you can misuse that free choice and that is what we are seeing today in the modern-day world. People have misused their free will. Instead of saying, "yes, I will surrender to God", they say "there is no God".

Or there is God but I am asking Him to be my order supplier. Give me, give me, give me. Here is my shopping list. The big amazon.com in the sky. Free delivery. Please give me amazon, God! This, this, this, this, this. So, it is time we wake up, become sober and realize the Supreme Personality of Godhead who is showing all kinds of special mercy when He comes and speaks the Bhagavad Gita. It is a very special blessing He is giving (**BG 18.66**)

sarva-dharmān parityajya
mām ekaṁ śaraṇaṁ vraja
ahaṁ tvāṁ sarva-pāpebhyo
mokṣayiṣyāmi mā śucaḥ

Give up all your nonsense and just fully surrender unto Me and I will alleviate you from all your sinful reactions. We have so many sinful reactions. This age is the age of sin, full of sinful activities. So, Krishna says, "Don't worry about all your sins. Just surrender and I will wipe out all your karmic reactions. You don't have to suffer the reactions of all your previous sins. Just surrender to Me".

But people are so foolish. They think God is just a myth and I am going to just try and enjoy, enjoy, enjoy, and they suffer like anything. They go down into the lower species in their next life. Now in Texas, there is so much anxiety. I have to be here and the electricity might be turned off and it is cold in my house. What about the poor animals? They are out in the cold all the time. The wild animals in the forest they have to go through the cold. The trees have to go through the cold. They don't get a warm house. So, we should be a little intelligent and realize I am getting a special facility as a human being to be more comfortable. Not that I always keep looking to eat, eat, eat, eat, and eat. The animals are constantly looking what can I eat? What can I eat? What can I eat? Human being has the facility to take care of his eating problem and then have so much free time. Instead of looking for self-realization in their free time, they want to go out and fly a kite. Or they want to go and get a motorcycle and do all kinds of unnecessary things. People have beyond their livelihood and their house duties, they have their hobbies, they want to go out and do so many things, surfing, they want to get very popular, in Hawaii especially, in southern California also they get the surfboards, Prabhupada called them sufferers instead of surfers, they are very fond of getting on that boards and riding the wave. It is all so nice! They get to ride on the waves. They are preparing themselves to become a fish in their next birth. The fish can get to ride the wave all the time. So, all these few hobbies we have for enjoying this way and enjoying that way in sense gratification is simply taking us down the animal kingdom. Some people like to skydive. They go up in an airplane and they have the parachute and they jump off the airplane and they just dive into the sky for some time, they fly around the sky thinking, "oh this is so wonderful" and right before they hit the ground, they open their parachutes. Sometimes, their parachute doesn't open and they get killed. They are willing to take the risk of not having their chute open and being smashed onto the ground so they can imitate the flying of the bird in the sky.

Real purpose of life:

So, one has to be intelligent and realize what is the real purpose of human life, not wasted running here and running there and trying to enjoy this, trying to enjoy that. Instead of trying to be the enjoyer of ourselves, we should try to serve the Supreme Enjoyer. That is the key. Many times, it has been explained, that when you water the root of the tree all the leaves and branches are nourished. When you feed the belly all the parts of the body are nourished. So, we have to try to give pleasure to that Supreme Person. He is the one meant to be the actual Enjoyer of everything.

bhoktāraṁ yajña-tapasāṁ
sarva-loka-maheśvaram
suhṛdaṁ sarva-bhūtānāṁ
jñātvā māṁ śāntim ṛcchati

(BG 5.29)

Krishna says that one who knows Me as the Owner of everything and as the Enjoyer of everything and the best friend of all living beings, he and only he can have peace of mind. So, those who try to be the enjoyer separately, cannot be happy. This is confirmed in the Bhagavad Gita. They can't be happy. They may think they are happy, but they are deluding themselves. They are not relishing the bliss of their spiritual identity. Anyone who tries to enjoy separately from the Lord is therefore forced to continue to misidentify themselves with their temporary rotting material body. It may seem very enjoyable when you are young and healthy, but when you get old and hit seventy the whole thing starts to fall apart. Where is the enjoyment? Well, they just think back to their childhood. Oh, I remember when I was a child, I was flying a kite, I was running here, running there, riding my bicycle around the block. The old people just try to remember when they were young and happy in the material world. Now they try to derive some pleasure. But why try to be happy artificially? All we have to do is get back to our own svarupa or original form. 'Sva' means own and 'rupa' is form, 'svarupa', our own identity. All we have to do is to get back to our original identity. Why should we try to squeeze pleasure out of false identities? *"punaḥ punaś carvita-carvaṇānām"* – we are trying to chew that has already been chewed. I try to enjoy in this material world in this way and that way and squeeze pleasures where I hardly got any pleasure but now, I am going to squeeze even harder and harder squeeze, squeeze, squeeze, squeeze, squeeze trying to get blood out of a rock. *"punaḥ punaś carvita-carvaṇānām"* – chewing that has already been chewed. They tried many times to get pleasure and they don't get any pleasure out of doing that thing but then I will do it again and maybe I will get pleasure this time and they try it again and again and again. In this way they become more and more frustrated and bewildered and go into states of depression. They go to the psychiatrist, to help them come out of depression because they have become so disenchanted, by any means they can be happy. Well, Krishna is the original psychiatrist. He is the real psychiatrist. The original psychiatric doctrine is the Bhagavad Gita. If we simply study the Bhagavad Gita, we can know how to simply become happy. Instead of misidentifying with that which is simply the source of misery and anxiety, we should get free from that misidentification and come back to our actual sat-chit-ananda vigraha identity – the eternal, knowledge and bliss. Isn't it a shame, isn't it pathetic that people are being trained in misidentifying the eternal, all-blissful, fully cognizant beings, who are being trained and programmed in misidentifying as that which is temporary, full of ignorance and misery? It is a crime and shame. But this is what all our leaders are doing. This is where our so-called leaders are taking us. These leaders are not leaders, they are simply cheaters. We need a new calibre of leadership on this planet, Krishna Conscious leadership. Actually, Prabhupada told us that. He said the day will come when we capture the government. Can you imagine? As our movement expands, eventually we will have Krishna Conscious governments on this planet. It is a great encouragement for us to preach and distribute books and cultivate and train people how to become pure devotees.

Because within this Chaitanya era there will be amazing flooding of this planet with Krishna consciousness, even the governments will be Krishna conscious, Prabhupada told that in one conversation. Always be enthusiastic and move forward, instead of becoming overwhelmed by all our defeats or mistakes. Instead, we should learn from our mistakes, but not have depression because of our mistakes. We should have a very positive forward-looking attitude, "Oh, I made this mistake, that mistake, let me learn from that mistake." Sometimes someone makes that mistake again. Let me move forward now to become more and more awakened in my Krishna consciousness. Even I was explaining to the devotees this morning at the end of the Japa period. There was somebody here for the Japa. What can I say? Prabhupada explains that one who purely chants the Holy Names of the Lord under his influence the whole world will take up the chanting of Hare Krishna. So, this is a very good reason for us, not only for our own liberation, to perfect our chanting but for the sake of deliverance of all the fallen souls of this world. Can you imagine everybody in the world will be chanting Hare Krishna wherever you went!

Hare Krishna Hare Krishna Krishna Krishna Hare Hare

Hare Rama Hare Rama Rama Rama Hare Hare

When the congress and the senate begin their daily sessions in Washington, "Hare Krishna Hare Krishna", when the United Nations gets together, 'Hare Krishna Hare Krishna", the British Parliament, and the Indian Parliament, and etc., when the people open their business or their shop every day or their corporation, "Hare Krishna Hare Krishna", even all the churches, mosques, and synagogues. Even if they chant Rama or Allah or Jehovah that is alright too. It is the same principle. Everybody should chant the Holy Names of God. If they think Hare Krishna is something Hindu, they can chant the name of Christ, or the name of Allah or the name of Jehovah, but let everybody vibrate the Holy Names of the Lord as a regular activity; their whole life is centred around it. That will eventually come on this planet. The whole world will be absorbed in chanting. Actually, Prabhupada said, they will chant Hare Krishna. Actually, it will come to the point that the whole world will chant Hare Krishna that's what is predicted. So, it is a very exciting future lying ahead. We should become very enthusiastic to make this whole world Krishna conscious as soon as possible. Preach, preach, preach to the world,

Prabhupada said, become very passive and enthusiastic to bring in Krishna conscious spiritual revolution to this planet ASAP.

Questions and Answers

VPM: We see, that the 10,000-year period that we mentioned will have an Indian summer.

SDA: Yes, like an Indian summer. When the winter comes there is a warm spell in the winter. It is a nice example that Gurumataji is giving us. It is like an Indian summer.

VPM: Like an Indian summer, Krishna consciousness will spread. Prabhupada did it. But after Prabhupada, it is becoming a little slack and everybody is going in the wrong direction. So, how we can expect that Indian summer will happen?

SDA: It is going to happen. That means at least one devotee, all it takes is one devotee who actually is purely practicing. Even if one person purely chants Hare Krishna, Prabhupada said, then he becomes a Jagad guru and under his influence, the whole world will chant Hare Krishna, even if there is only one follower of Prabhupada who does it. But I think we can have thousands of followers of Prabhupada who can purely chant the Holy name. But even if there is only one that's all it takes to keep it going. Even if there is one person who can keep it going.

VPM: But those who were with Prabhupada they are dying off and the young ones it is becoming a little watered down.

SDA: Watered down means *nama aparadha*. That is what watered down means.

VPM: Then how can we expect that even one will come?

SDA: Each one of us should try to be that one. I should try to be that one person and you should try to be that one person.

VPM: But you will be dying now.

SDA: I am training my disciples. They should also try to be that one person who can purely chant the Holy names to influence the whole world to chant 'Hare Krishna'. All my disciples must become pure chanters of the Holy Names. That is my order to all my disciples. They should all become pure chanters of the Holy Name so that even any one of them can deliver the whole world. That is my order to all my disciples.

So, don't give in to your senses. Don't engage in illicit activities. If you are married don't have sex for recreation. If you are married, you only have sex when you are trying to have a child after you have chanted 50 rounds of Japa.

VPM: But you are the only one out of that. Because nowadays that is allowed. Because many times Prabhupada said that outside marriage. So, they are arguing.

SDA: Well, tonight I am playing a lecture from Prabhupada during the dressing of the Deity, Srimad Bhagavatam 1.3.17. You can hear what Prabhupada said about married life very clearly. I am playing that lecture this evening. It is a lecture on First Canto, chapter 3 text number 17. Prabhupada gives all kinds of talk about married life, and what is the proper mood for married life.

VPM: But that is only sometimes. But mostly he said the other way around. So, which should we choose?

SDA: Prabhupada never says you can have sex for recreation. He never said that. Not in one place, he said you can have sex for recreation.

VPM: Within marriage and outside marriage?

SDA: He never said you can have sex for recreation within marriage. Never. Show me one place where Prabhupada said that if you are married now you can enjoy sex without restriction. Not even in one place Prabhupada said that. He never said that if you are married and you can have sex with your wife without restriction. He never said that.

VPM: Then how come our leaders are saying that?

SDA: If some leader is saying that if you are married then you can have sex as much as you want, just abort the child. If someone is saying then they are wrong. All I can say is they are off track and they have deviated from Prabhupada.

Nandini: Hare Krishna Gurudeva. If somehow the whole world would become Krishna conscious, then can we avoid the disastrous outcome of Kali-yuga?

SDA: No. It is already there. Prabhupada said after the 10,000 years the whole world is filled with no more devotees. No more Hare Krishna. There will be a full facility for meat-eating. "I eat you or you eat me". Even they will eat their own children just like snakes sometimes eat their own children. People at the end of the ten thousand years period, they will be eating their own children. That is how much they will be degraded. They will eat their own children. There won't be any more Hare Krishnas. All devotees will be back home back to Godhead and Kalki avatar will come and annihilate all those rascals to bring in the Satya yuga. Not that it is not going to happen. The scriptures don't lie. What is stated in the scriptures is going to happen Nandini. So, you become very fixed up so you are not here to see the fun when the Kalki avatar has to come.

Bhakta Ravi Kolluru: If somebody is a sea-surfer or a sky-diver before they come to Krishna consciousness, can they use their skill to attract people who are adventurous to come to Krishna consciousness?

SDA: It could be done. You could do a publicity stunt. If you are a skydiver and as you are landing this huge flag of Hare Krishna mahamantra comes out so all people can see it. Do you know any sky divers in our movement? You could use it as a publicity stunt to attract people to Krishna consciousness. It could be done.

VPM: So, does that mean that the Hare Krishna mahamantra is not powerful to attract people but sky diving is more powerful that it will attract people. Does that what it means?

SDA: No.

Bhadra devi dasi: Is the control of the material nature been allotted to the demigods?

SDA: Yes, that is right. They are His assistants in controlling material nature. That is right.

Ok, our time is up, does anyone have any more questions? Gurumataji, you like to make some corrections or some complaints?

VPM: Yes. I just said that do we have to use the sense gratification method to attract people?

SDA: Not required actually. We already have our books, we have our kirtan, we have our lectures. That is our basic formula. Prasadam distribution, Harinam sankirtan, book distribution. These are the primary means of pushing forward this movement. Ok, now we have Bhakta Ravi Kolluru.

Ravi Kolluru: I don't know of any skydivers yet but in the future, if I meet anyone, I can use them for Hare Krishna publicity stunt if they are willing to do it.

SDA: Ok

VPM: Is the Hare Krishna not powerful enough Bhakta Ravi Kolluru? Isn't the Hare Krishna mantra strong enough that we need skydivers to promote Hare Krishna?

SDA: Actually, we teach everyone to be a sky flyer. The skydivers want to fly in the sky. But we are teaching everyone how to be a sky flyer. When you chant Hare Krishna, Hare Krishna, Krishna Krishna, Hare Hare, Hare Rama, Hare Rama, Rama Rama, Hare Hare, you are flying in the spiritual sky. Divers mean they come back down to the earth but we don't come back down to the earth. This mantra will take you higher and higher. It is a sky flyer, not a skydiver. Skydiver means they come back down to the earth. We don't come down. We just go up, up, up, up back to Krishna, back home back to Godhead.

Bahurupa Chaitanya das: [From Chile] Even though one is polluted by the Mayavada philosophy, how can one please Guru and the Lord?

SDA: You have to give up the Mayavada philosophy. Mayavada philosophy means you think you are God. You have to kick out Mayavada philosophy and teach them they are not God.

Bhaktin Angala Parameshwari: How to understand if a person is doing the wrong things? Do the activities depend on my previous karma and due to the contamination of this kali yuga too?

SDA: We have the scriptures to tell us what is right and what is wrong. Scriptures are our law books. It is very simple the scriptures tell us what is proper action and what is improper action.

Bahurupa Chaitanya das: What am I? I have not much intelligence.

SDA: Well, that is the beginning of intelligence Bahurupa. When you understand that I have not much intelligence, now your intelligence has begun. If you think, "Oh I am very intelligent" that means you are a fool and rascal. When you say, "I don't have much intelligence I am simply a fool and rascal". Now you have some intelligence but keep that mood I have no intelligence and always depend on Guru and Krishna to enlighten me. Then you become the most intelligent person in the whole universe.

Bhakta Ravi Kolluru: Hare Krishna mantra is powerful but if somebody has some extraordinary skills can they be used also?

SDA: Anybody whatever talents they have if they can use it for propagating Krishna consciousness then do it.

VPM: But, if we chant Hare Krishna, what else do we need? Like you said even if one person can chant Hare Krishna purely then they can go back home back to Godhead.

SDA: Very good point. Not that we need so many techniques. Pure chanting itself actually will have an impact on the whole universe. Very good point.

Sanat Kumar das: Is learning about the bodily chakras important for Krishna consciousness practice?

SDA: No. It is absolutely not necessary. No need to worry about the bodily chakras. Just be concerned *Hare Krishna, Hare Krishna, Krishna Krishna, Hare Hare / Hare Rama, Hare Rama, Rama Rama, Hare Hare.*

You will be on all the chakras.

So, we will go ahead and stop here. We thank everybody for tuning in.

Hare Krishna Hare Krishna Krishna Krishna Hare Hare

Hare Rama Hare Rama Rama Rama Hare Hare

If you want to enjoy genuine happiness and not be a miserable fool like 99.99% of the world population, you need to tune in, turn on, and bliss out. Tune in to Krishna. Turn on your true spiritual identity. And bliss out by surfing on the waves of Lord Caitanya's unlimited mercy. You've nothing to lose except for your ignorance and anxiety. So, why not do it right now?

-Monday 28 Mar 2016-

Lesson 4

TELL EVERYBODY ABOUT KRISHNA.

~~~ ~~~ ~~~

Srimad Bhagavatam 3.29.15

Austin, Texas

Date: 22-JAN-2021

Om Namo Bhagavate Vasudevaya

[Gurudeva sings three times and devotees repeat]

niṣevitenānimittena
sva-dharmeṇa mahīyasā
kriyā-yogena śastena
nātihiṁsreṇa nityaśaḥ

Synonyms

niṣevitena — executed; *animittena* — without attachment to the result; *sva-dharmeṇa* — by one's prescribed duties; *mahīyasā* — glorious; *kriyā-yogena* — by devotional activities; *śastena* — auspicious; *na* — without; *atihiṁsreṇa* — excessive violence; *nityaśaḥ* — regularly.

violence; *nityasaḥ* — regularly.

Translation

"A devotee must execute his prescribed duties, which are glorious, without material profit. Without excessive violence, one should regularly perform one's devotional activities."

Purport

One has to execute his prescribed duties according to his social position as a brahmana, ksatriya, vaisya or sudra. The prescribed duties of the four classes of men in human society are also described in Bhagavad-gita. The activities of Brahmanas are to control the senses and to become simple, clean, learned devotees. The ksatriyas have the spirit for ruling, they are not afraid on the battlefield, and they are charitable. The vaisyas, or the mercantile class of men, trade in commodities, protect cows and develop agricultural produce. The sudras, or laborer class, serve the higher classes because they themselves are not very intelligent.

From every position, as confirmed in Bhagavad-gita, *sva-karmana tam abhyarcya:* one can serve the Supreme Lord by performing one's prescribed duty. It is not that only the brahmanas can serve the Supreme Lord and not the sudras. Anyone can serve the Supreme Lord by performing his prescribed duties under the direction of a spiritual master, or representative of the Supreme Personality of Godhead. No one should think that his prescribed duties are inferior. A brahmana can serve the Lord by using his intelligence, and the ksatriya can serve the Supreme Lord by using his military arts, just as Arjuna served Krishna. Arjuna was a warrior; he had no time to study Vedanta or other highly intellectual books. The damsels in Vrajadhama were girls born of the Vaisya class, and they engaged in protecting cows and producing agriculture. Krishna's foster father, Nanda Maharaja, and his associates were all vaisyas. They were not at all educated, but they could serve Krishna by loving Him and by offering everything to Him. Similarly, there are many instances in which candalas, or those lower than sudras, have served Krishna. Also, the sage Vidura was considered a sudra because his mother happened to be a sudra. There are no distinctions, for it is declared by the Lord in Bhagavad-gita that anyone engaged specifically in devotional service is elevated to the transcendental position without a doubt. Everyone's prescribed duty is glorious if it is performed in the devotional service of the Lord, without desire for profit. Such loving service must be performed without reason, without impediment, and spontaneously. Krishna is lovable, and one has to serve Him in whatever capacity one can. That is pure devotional service.

Another significant phrase in this verse is *natihimsrena,* "with minimum violence or sacrifice of life." Even if a devotee has to commit violence, it should not be done beyond what is necessary. Sometimes the question is put before us: "You ask us not to eat meat, but you are eating vegetables. Do you think that is not violence?" The answer is that eating vegetables is violence, and vegetarians are also committing violence against other living entities because vegetables also have life. Non-devotees are killing cows, goats and so many other animals for eating purposes, and a devotee, who is vegetarian, is also killing. But here, significantly, it is stated that every living entity has to live by killing another entity; that is the law of nature. *Jivo jivasya jivanam:* one living entity is the life for another living entity. But for a human being, that violence should be committed only as much as necessary.

A human being is not to eat anything which is not offered to the Supreme Personality of Godhead. *Yajna-sistasinah santah:* one becomes freed from all sinful reactions by eating foodstuffs which are offered to Yajna, the Supreme Personality of Godhead. A devotee therefore eats only *prasada,* or foodstuffs offered to the Supreme Lord, and Krishna says that when a devotee offers Him foodstuffs from the vegetable kingdom, with devotion, He eats that. A devotee is to offer to Krishna foodstuffs prepared from vegetables. If the Supreme Lord wanted foodstuffs prepared from animal food, the devotee could offer this, but He does not order to do that.

We have to commit violence; that is a natural law. We should not, however, commit violence extravagantly, but only as much as ordered by the Lord. Arjuna engaged in the art of killing, and although killing is, of course, violence, he killed the enemy simply on Krishna's order. In the same way, if we commit violence as it is necessary, by the order of the Lord, that is called *natihimsa.* We cannot avoid violence, for we are put into a conditional life in which we have to commit violence, but we should not commit more violence than necessary or than ordered by the Supreme Personality of Godhead. (End of Purport)

Sankarshan das Adhikari:

Prabhupada first talks about the different social orders, the *brahmanas*, *ksatriyas*, *vaisyas*, and *sudras*. Nowadays, as stated in the Vedic wisdom, "*Kalau sudra sambhavah*" – in this age of Kali, everyone is a sudra. There are a few *vaisyas*, a few shopkeepers, and a few farmers here and there but the vast majority of people are *sudra* class. They don't have any own intelligence to start their own business or to be a proper administrator of the society or to be a learned *brahmana*, they don't have the intelligence to do that. All they know is how to do is work a job, and get a job. Even though they are highly educated, even though they have a Ph. D. degree, if they can't get find employment, they are in great difficulty. Today we have no real *ksatriyas*. These so-called political leaders, they are just *sudras* basically, elevated *sudras*, worker class. We have no actual administrators, *ksatriyas* like Yudhisthira Maharaj or Arjuna, who are duty bound to protect the citizens, even the animals being unnecessarily harmed. You have the Presidents, Prime Ministers, all eating meat, sitting there and eating meat in the White House or wherever they may be, eating hamburgers, fried chicken and so many things, this is not *ksatriya*. *Ksatriya* protects every citizen, even the animal citizens within his kingdom. As far as *brahmanas*, we have so-called *brahmanas*, they are all eating meat. They are all engaged in sinful activities, so-called college professors, priests, rabbis, they are all engaged in nonsense. Sometimes I use to go to see my minister. When I was a young Christian boy, I remember visiting my minister in his what is called pastor's study, his office of the church, I saw him smoking a big cigar. The other one, before him, he was smoking a pipe. They were seen around smoking. This is the *brahmana* class smoking? Our Krishna consciousness movement is meant to establish actual *Brahmanas*, and *Ksatriyas*, we want to establish as well. We want to establish a class of *Brahmanas* and *Ksatriyas*. Then the society will become very nice, we can educate everyone on how to utilize their occupational tendencies, in the service of the Lord, even the *sudras* can be nicely engaged. They are all engaged in Krishna's service, they become also great devotees. Not that everyone has to be a *Brahmana*, or *Ksatriya* or *Vaisya*. Everybody can be engaged according to their natural propensity. In this way, they can all become glorious and they can all go back to home, back to Godhead upon leaving their present body. Prabhupada talks a lot here about the unnecessary violence being committed against the animals. Krishna says,

> *patraṁ puṣpaṁ phalaṁ toyaṁ*
> *yo me bhaktyā prayacchati*
> *tad ahaṁ bhakty-upahṛtam*
> *aśnāmi prayatātmanaḥ*

"If one offers Me with love and devotion a leaf, a flower, a fruit or water, I will accept it." (BG 9.26)

There is a leaf, a flower, a fruit, or water, there is no mention of meat. If Krishna had said, "Offer Me meat." Then we could offer Him meat, but He asks only for vegetarian foodstuffs. The point here is, that is also killing, so that is also violence. When you pull a carrot out of the ground, you just killed a carrot. It's a living being in a carrot's body, you uproot the carrot, and now you are killing him. It is still living for a little while because you can put that carrot in some water and it will grow. But then you started cutting it up, peeling it, and cutting it up. It's finished. We are allowed to do a certain amount of violence according to Krishna's instructions. The *Ksatriya's* are also allowed to kill the aggressors. For those who are committing unnecessary violence, the *Ksatriyas* can use violence to curb them down. In this way, even violence can be used for Krishna's service. How many people were killed in the battlefield of Kuruksetra. That's under Krishna's order. "Rise now and fight the battle."

Some people think it's just an allegory. But no, that's an actual battle. So many warriors were killed on that battlefield on Krishna's order. When violence is required, Krishna will engage the devotee in committing violence. I remember years ago, our temples were sometimes being robbed and attacked. Different robberies were going on. Prabhupada said, "give me a gun in one hand and bead bag in another, I will protect you". That was what Prabhupada said. We had a robbery there in our Miami temple. They came with rifles and pistols to rob us. We had a gun there. That was quite an interesting evening. In the evening we all get together for milk prasadam. It's a nice time at the end of the day we all sit around and have some milk prasadam. But all of a sudden, into the prasadam room, comes two bandits. One of them had a gun at Bhaktin Paddy's head, the other had a big rifle. He said, "everybody get down on the floor". Bhaktin Paddy was going like "Ahh.." She was in great anxiety that they are going to shoot her. They threatened us to get down on the floor, but I was thinking what is this nonsense "get down on the floor. I am not going to bow down to these guys, these rascals." I just yelled out "Narasimhadev". Narasimhadev is the great protector, so I yelled out "Narasimhadev". Now the gun is no longer pointed to Bhaktin Paddy, it's pointed to me. I thought, well I am going to negotiate with them. "We are your friends. What do you want?" He said "The money, where is the money?" At that point our temple President came walking in, out of the treasury, which is adjoining the prasadam room, to take milk prasadam. He was a little surprised to see robbery going on in the prasadam room. All bandits had rifles and pistols. He decided to go back to the treasury where there was a gun. We had a gun to protect ourselves from violence. The temple President said, "Get the gun and shoot the bastard." He told to the treasurer. So, violence can be used. These people threatened to kill us. In that situation you could use violence, you can kill them if necessary. "Get the gun and shoot the bastard." He told him. As soon as they heard this, they went running scared. And the temple treasurer came out and "boom" He shot at them.

Violence can be used in Krishna's service, even as devotees we can use violence if we have to shoot somebody, we can do that if necessary. Temple President told to shoot them, it's self-defense. Violence can be used in Krishna's service. Even though we are nonviolent by nature, but for protection's sake, violence can be used.

Anything can be used in Krishna's service. Whatever is necessary, we can use it for Krishna. Right now, the whole world is in great suffering condition due to the lack of Krishna consciousness. So, we have to use any or all means to awaken them to Krishna consciousness. This is what Prabhupada wants us to do, he wants us to make the whole world Krishna conscious.

Prabhupada very much recognized me when I was a young *brahmacari* because I had this desire to make the world Krishna conscious. He even wrote me a nice letter encouraging me in that mood. After my initiation, I sent some Guru daksina to London. I sent him a letter on 2nd September 1971. That was amazing, only 5 days later, Prabhupada replied, which means the letter crossed the Atlantic very quickly. Only 5 days later, he wrote me a reply from London. In that letter, he said, "I can see that you are a very sincere and enthusiastic boy, anxious to spread this movement. Those are first-class qualifications for making advancement in Krishna consciousness. So continue enthusiastically as you are doing and surely Krishna will bless you." Prabhupada very much liked our wanting to spread this movement. He recognized me that I was wanting to spread this Krishna consciousness movement.

We have to have this desire. Not just my own Krishna consciousness, a devotee is compassionate. He sees the suffering world around him, all hell is breaking loose, just like it happened in Washington DC because there is no proper leadership. We want to establish proper leadership. Prabhupada said we need to establish *brahmanas* and *ksatriyas*. We have to establish these two classes. We need to have proper leadership. How do we establish Ksatriyas in today's democracy? We have to educate the voters. We have to do massive book distribution and all kinds of preaching. Everything we can do to flood this world with Krishna consciousness, so people will understand. They may not be devotees yet, but they will understand that many devotee leaders. They may not be fully ready to take up the process, but they can understand that these Hare Krishna people they have the proper understanding of how this world can be properly managed in such a way that everybody is happy. "Let these Hare Krishna people be the leaders of the world". We need to preach in such a way that people will want Krishna conscious leaders in the Whitehouse, in Buckingham palace, the parliament building, and in every place in the world they want Krishna conscious leadership. We have to preach in such a way that people will vote for Krishna conscious leaders because this will bring to end all the strife that is going on in the world. It's horrible strife that is going on. People don't realize how wonderful is Krishna and these amazing pastimes of Krishna, and amazing teachings of Krishna, we have to bring Krishna to the forefront. His teachings, it's so full of mercy so full of love, and transcendental pastimes.

Just like I was reading this morning, Krishna was in the house of Radharani. He is in Radharani's house and Radharani's husband comes back. Radharani's husband Abhimanyu. Here He is with another man's wife. Radharani is actually married to Abhimanyu. Krishna there He is in the house of Radharani, Abhimanyu is coming back, so what to do? Krishna is so clever, He disguised Himself as Abhimanyu and He addresses Jatila, the mother. The mother is also there. Now He is dressed as Abhimanyu. He addresses Jatila, the mother. The mother is also there. Now He is dressed as Abhimanyu. He says "O My dear mother I am your real son Abhimanyu, but just see Krishna dressed up like Me is coming before you." [Laughs] The actual Abhimanyu is actually Krishna disguised as Abhimanyu. "I am the real Abhimanyu and Abhimanyu is Krishna disguised as Abhimanyu." So Jatila believes Krishna thinking this is her actual son and she becomes angry at her real son Abhimanyu who is coming home now. "Who is this?" She becomes angry at him and is driving him away. "Get out of here, get out of here." She is driving the actual Abhimanyu thinking him to be Krishna. And Abhimanyu is crying " Mother Mother what are you doing?" The girlfriends of Radharani are there, just laughing and smiling.

Just an amazing Personality, His wonderful teachings, these amazing pastimes which are so attractive. We have to distribute these books of Srila Prabhupada so that people can get attracted to the pastimes of Krishna. Now they are reading about the rockstar, the movie star. What are these rascal characters? They are just greedy people. They are not really attractive people. We have a desire to be attracted to a hero. It's our natural tendency. Because we are all devotees of Krishna, we have a tendency to be attracted to Krishna and the great sages. When we get covered by the material energy, we take that tendency and we get attracted to a movie star, musicians, politicians, the actors etc. These people are actually disgusting. Just like when I was a kid, a big hero during my days was the singer named Bob Dylan, a big hero. He was considered a great hero of the counterculture. He made so much money by selling his music, now he sold his whole music catalog for 300 million dollars. He is just after money. He is a greedy person but he is made into a big hero. It's a shame actually that people are running after these musicians, politicians, and actors thinking them to be great heroes. Actually, they are just greedy envious people. We need to take this tendency and to repose it in Krishna. That's why we have these books, the Krishna book, Nectar of Devotion is full of so many amazing pastimes, we should read these pastimes and become attracted to these pastimes. So many amazing pastimes like Hiranyakasipu and Nrsimhdeva, such an amazing thing. Hiranyakasipu wants to achieve immortality. He wants to become immortal. He worships Lord Brahma to get benediction of immortality, and he actually does all these austerities and penances, now he thinks he has got it. Brahma actually tricks him. You will not die in the day or night, you will not die in the land or sea, you will not be killed by any man or beast, by any weapon, in this way he gives all these boons and now Hiranyakasipu is like "Now I am immortal, I am immortal, I am immortal." But then Krishna appears as Narasimhadev, He kills him in the twilight, not in the day or night, He doesn't kill him with any weapon, He kills Him with the nails of His hands, He was not killed by a man or beast, He was killed by a half man and half beast. In this way, Krishna is so clever, He outsmarts these demons every time.

We shouldn't be fooled by these nonsense rascal demons, these material scientists, the big bang, everything came out of an explosion, can you imagine how idiotic that is, to say that this beautiful universe, the lotus flower was caused by an explosion. Explosions don't create order; they break down the order. We are supposed to believe these scientists who say that everything came out of an explosion, a big bang. It's time we stop putting out faith in these rascals, it's time we stop putting our faith on these mudhas, these rascals, these idiots, and put our faith on those persons who actually have knowledge like Srila Vyasadev, the great Vaisnava Acaryas, Krishna Himself. It's time we put our faith and take knowledge from those persons who know things as they are. If you want to know something about something, the person who invented it, he is the knower. Just like someone makes some invention, they are the best knower of that invention, isn't it? Why not see, who is the person who invented the reality we are living in? Who is the creator of it? That's Krishna. Why don't we go to Krishna? Krishna is the Supreme authority. Krishna knows everything, past, present, and future. Why don't we put our faith in Krishna instead of our rascal mind, these rascal scientists, we should put our faith in Krishna. Krishna is the perfect knower of everything. "My dear Lord, I humbly submit myself unto You. You kindly enlighten me, kindly deliver me from the illusion, I am caught up in right now." In this way, we can actually make our lives perfect.

We can derive unlimited satisfaction and bliss and we can actually turn this world into a paradise. There is no reason for us to suffer like this. Prabhupada actually told us, he said, "If you simply read, chant, and preach as much as possible, then very soon this Krishna consciousness movement will be accepted as the only religion in this world." Can you imagine? If Hare Krishna, Krishna consciousness was universally accepted as the world religion, in every town, village, city, and hamlet in the entire world, can you imagine how wonderful it would be? Prabhupada said we can do it. We can accomplish that, we simply have to read, chant and preach as much as possible every day. Read these books, keep reading, every spare minute you have, read, read, read these books. There are so many books written by devotees also. Just like right now, I have a book sitting in the kitchen. In the middle of my service, I get the offering ready, there are a few minutes left before the arati, if I have 2 or 3 minutes, I pick up that book. I am right now reading about the devotees who were put in prison in Russia during the Soviet era. They were being tortured like hell in the prison; it's horrible what they were going through. They were beaten severely. They told how they were living in the prison. Many devotees were put in the different cells throughout the prison. On Gaura Purnima, somehow they had little money, they bribed the guard and let him do a kirtan. They were all singing the most glorious kirtan throughout the whole jail, singing on Gaura purnima. Actually they didn't know when is Gaura Purnima. Some mataji came snuck in near the prison, got to the window, and yelled at them what day it was for Gaura Purnima. Then they all knew when is Gaura Purnima." They went through hell. These guards sometimes would come and beat them so they would be in pain for days. They were beaten severely by the guards; they went through so much hell but still they maintained their Krishna consciousness. It's an amazing story of how they survived living in the prison. The guards were very cruel and they would beat them again and again, it's amazing how they survived in the prison. There are so many wonderful books out there written by devotees also, you can read them as well. Our main curriculum is Prabhupada books. Then we have the extracurricular books as well. Just like I just finished reading the book written by Mukunda Maharaj "Happiness at Second Avenue", about how the movement began. It's amazing how Prabhupada started this movement. He had no proper facility, living in the bowery where the drunks were passing urine, and vomiting in the whole way, it was horrible what Prabhupada went through. It's an amazing story, it's history. We can read Prabhupada's books, other books written by devotees. We can read, we can hear lectures, we can chant, we can memorize verses, we can chant Brahma samhita, we can chant different verses, and we can sing beautiful songs by the Vaisnava acaryas, there is so much to do to absorb ourselves 24/7, constantly hearing about, reading about and preaching the glories of Krishna. Take every opportunity to preach to the world. Krishna blessed me yesterday. A very favorable person who asked me and he wanted to know about Krishna consciousness, it was a very big radio show, on 14 stations it went live yesterday afternoon. We should take every opportunity to preach, and tell people about Krishna wherever we can. Go to meetings, go to street corners, go everywhere you can, go on the internet, wherever you can, tell your neighbors, tell your friends, tell your relatives, tell everybody you can, about Krishna. We want to revolutionize this planet; we have to tell everybody about Krishna.

yare dekha, tare kaha 'krsna'-upadesa

amara ajnaya guru hana tara 'ei desa

(CC Madhya 7.128)

Whomever you meet, instruct them in the teachings of Krishna. In this way on My order, you become guru and you deliver this world. Is this only for the spiritual master and initiating gurus? No. This is for every rank-and-file member of ISKCON. You become guru. Everyone is meant to be a siksha guru, one who instructs others. Everyone in our movement is meant to be a siksha guru. Even the children, everyone should become siksha guru.

Question and Answers:

Alakananda: Does the word "learned" in the purport indicate having spiritual knowledge or material knowledge?

SDA: What paragraph is it in? I don't know. I don't have time to look through it. Let me know what paragraph it is in. There are different kinds of "learned", let me know what paragraph it is in. Give me the whole quote. Just type in the whole sentence, that should be the best thing. So I don't have to look for it.

Mahabhagavat - We say in Bhagavad Gita that varna, caste depends on qualities, guna and karma. Vidura was the highest category of saint so why was he considered *sudra*.

SDA: - Because his mother happened to be a *sudra*. He was born in *sudra* family. That's why he is considered as *sudra* in one sense, it's described in the purport.

Mahabhagavat - The description doesn't make sense.

SDA- Well, how can you say that what Prabhupada says doesn't make sense? That doesn't make sense to me Mahabhagavat. You would say that what Prabhupada has written doesn't make sense, you can say, you can't understand it. It doesn't make sense to you, but you can't say, it's a nonsensical statement. There is a difference. It doesn't make sense to you, but you can't say it's a nonsensical statement. In Vedic culture that was generally the system. In Vedic culture that was how it worked because by association those born of a *sudra* family were *sudras* naturally because the qualities were passed on. In previous ages, that was the system. It was based on birth not by force but by the qualities. Because you are associating with that varna, you will naturally have that varna by that association those qualities will develop in you too. That was formally how it worked. In this kali yuga, it's quite different. In this yuga everyone is sudra. *Kalau sudra sambhava*. But Lord Caitanya's movement will elevate them from their lower position to brahminical stage, by association, by the power of the Holy names. It's from a previous yuga. Vidura is a brahmana in the sense of being a Vaisnava. A Vaisnava is automatically a brahmana, even though externally he may act as a ksatriya or a vaisya or a sudra. A Vaisnava is naturally a brahmana automatically, even though externally he may act differently in the society.

Mahabhagavat - We give the example of Dronacarya who acted as a *ksatriya*, Parasurama who acted as a *ksatriya* and the son of a prostitute who acted as a *brahmana*, therefor this is inconsistent.

SDA – Interesting! We need to study. I wouldn't accuse Prabhuapda of inconsistency. I can't. You are merging into a little dangerous territory Mahabhagavat. You can't say, "O Prabhupada, your writing is inconsistent." You have to go to deeper level, that's all I can say. Go to a deeper level.

Sadhu Bhusana - It worked with other yugas because the goal of whole society was to satisfy Krishna. *Hari tosanam.*

SDA – That's a comment.

Mahabhagavat - Please help me go to the deeper level Srila Gurudev. What is the proper understanding here?

SDA - We all have to go to deeper level. I can't give you an intellectual answer for that. Why in this sense Vidura is considered a *sudra*? Wait a minute. Here is one-point Mahabhagavt. It doesn't say Vidura was a *sudra*, he was considered a *sudra* from an external viewpoint. That's an easy answer. Prabhupada doesn't say he was a *sudra*, he was considered as sudra.

Bhaktin Angalaparameshwari - A person who is doing a kind of corrupt activity, but still he is offering the results to the Lord, does he get purification?

SDA- Sure. Just like some thief robs a bank, but he gives part of his plundered funds as donation to ISKCON, we are not telling people to do this, it's just an example. Yes, he will get benefit. Of course, we shouldn't go and rob banks. But if the bank robber gives some portion of his robbery to Krishna, that's for his benefit.

Hare Krishna Das - Can one love and appreciate devotees by loving Krishna or it is vice-verse?

SDA - It actually works both ways. If someone is attracted to Krishna and then he finds someone who is also attracted to Krishna... Birds of same feather flock together, right? If you are attracted to Krishna and you find someone who is also attracted to Krishna, you will be like "Oh you are attracted to Krishna?" So it works both ways. Someone is attracted to devotees, then they find out that devotees are attracted to Krishna. So it works both ways.

Devotee - Qualities of a *brahmana*?

SDA –

> *śamo damas tapaḥ śaucaṁ*
> *kṣāntir ārjavam eva ca*
> *jñānaṁ vijñānam āstikyaṁ*
> *brahma-karma svabhāva-jam*

(BG 18.42)

There is jnana and vijnana. A Brahmana has both. He is learned in spiritual knowledge. And vijnana means he is an expert in applying the knowledge also. If you simply have theoretical knowledge but you don't apply it, then you are not really on the brahminical platform. The quality of a brahmana is jnana vijnyanam, practical application. He has great spiritual knowledge; at the same time, he applies that knowledge. It's not just theoretical. He puts it into practice. And here is an insider's secret, Alakananda. If you don't really apply this knowledge, you lose it in due course of time, it goes in and out. If you actually apply the knowledge, then it becomes realized knowledge. Otherwise, theoretical knowledge comes and goes, you can't keep it. But when you apply it, that applied knowledge becomes realized. So you have to take the theoretical knowledge, the learning you have and you have to apply it. Just like it's stated,

'sādhu-saṅga', 'sādhu-saṅga' — sarva-śāstre
kaya
lava-mātra sādhu-saṅge sarva-siddhi haya

(CC Madhya 22.054)

By association with the sadhus, one achieves perfection. One should take the association of the devotees. We have our programs here in Austin which are very safe. We have them outside, not inside, where everybody is at a great distance from one another. So, it's very safe. One should come to these programs. Sastra says, by associating with devotees one achieves *sarva-siddhi haya,* one achieves all perfection. "Well, I am learned because I know this verse." But if you are aloof from devotee association, then that knowledge is lost but if you apply that knowledge, vijnanam, then you achieve all perfection. Being learned is very good but if you don't apply it, you lose that learning in due course of time. When you apply it, it becomes very powerful, it becomes realized knowledge.

Bhaktin Priya Balani - What is my prescribed duty?

SDA - In this movement we are creating *brahmanas*. You are enrolled in *brahmana* school, we are training you on how to become a *brahmana*. That's what you have to do. We are creating *brahmanas*, you learn how to become a *brahmana*.

Bhaktin Shivani- Does being Krishna Consciousness means to be single-minded?

SDA - Yes, one-pointed determination. "I must become a pure devotee of Krishna." Here is what Prabhupada told us in Los Angeles, he said, "Become perfect and become a leader of the world." That's our duty, to become perfect and become a leader of the world. A world leader means preacher, one who shows an ideal example and one who teaches others how to be the ideal example. That's called world leader. Someone who is leading the world by their example. So Prabhupada told us that's a one-pointed thing, "be perfect and be a world leader. That's our one-pointed determination.

Amala Purana - We get so much knowledge from all different fields of devotional service from Bhagavad Gita and Srimad Bhagavatam. Please help us understand, how we can practically follow what we are reading from these books. Is our daily practice of chanting, following regulative principles, eating prasadam can be called a practical application of knowledge?

SDA - Yes. Sadhana bhakti – hearing, chanting, remembering, offering prayers, these activities, *nava vidha bhakti*. s*ravana, kirtana, smarana, and vandana* in this way, these 9 activities of bhakti. That is the practical application of what we are reading. Hear about Krishna, talk about Krishna, bow down to Krishna, offer prayers to Krishna, everything for Krishna's service 24/7.

Devotee - When we preach some of the people are willing material benefits from us. How to deal with them?

SDA - They want material benefits from us, how to deal with them? I understand what you are saying. People want blessings for "I am looking for a new job, please bless me that I can get a good job." Some of them come to devotees with those kinds of ideas. We should preach to them if you want to be situated in happiness, you want to be successful and happy in life, right? If you focus on surrendering yourself to Krishna, just like it is stated in the Bible, "Seek ye first the kingdom of God; and all other things shall be added unto you". If you put Krishna first, everything else follows automatically. Success and happiness follow automatically, to one who puts Krishna first. If you want success and happiness without Krishna, good luck. OK.

Lila Manjari - Is causing anxiety to others also considered violence?

SDA - It depends. If they are in anxiety because you are Krishna conscious, then no, just like some parents get into anxiety when their children want to become devotees. My mother was in anxiety about it. She would bring me a Bible and give me the points. "Son, remember you are baptized Christian, why you are giving up Jesus." [laughs] She was in anxiety. My dad was cool, but my mother was not cool with me being Krishna conscious. That wasn't violence simply to chant Hare Krishna and become a disciple of Srila Prabhupada. So it depends on what kind of anxiety you are causing them. If we are offensive towards Vaisnavas, if we are not properly behaving when we are associating with devotees and they are in anxiety because of our being offensive, then that is violence. Being offensive, Vaisnava aparadha is a subtle form of violence.

Lila Manjari - Knowingly or unknowingly we are causing anxiety to many living entities, how to get over it?

SDA - Always be in the mood of loving service, serving the Vaisnavas, even one must avoid jiva aparadha, being offensive to any living entity. Our mood is to give service to everyone, to be Krishna conscious, and help everybody connect with Krishna. That's the proper mood.

Paramatma Dasa - Some devotees treat different devotees differently not being equipoised, does that mean they are committing violence by showing partiality?

SDA- Yes, we should not do party politics with devotees. We should be equipoised, that devotee is the well-wishing friend of all living entities. That's the position of a devotee. To distinguish – "This person I like, that person I don't like." Just like the brahmacharis are great, but women are just a bunch of prostitutes. One has to be equipoised. No, they are your mothers. Treat them respectfully, they are your mothers. Thank you everybody for tuning in. *Hare Krishna Hare Krishna Krishna Krishna Hare Hare, Hare Rama Hare Rama, Rama Rama Hare Hare.*

In material society, intoxication is indeed very, very popular. It's so popular that it is a multi-billion dollar industry. But no matter how much a person gets intoxicated, the effect of the intoxicant will eventually wear off and he or she will have to deal with the miseries and anxieties of normal everyday waking reality again.

However, if one is Krishna conscious, he stays high forever with no coming down. In this state of divine intoxication, we are not dull-headed. Rather we are blessed with sharp ever-increasing intelligence, compassion, joyfulness, and alertness. This is why a divinely intoxicated person, a Krishna conscious person, can easily give up all forms of mundane intoxication as easily as a pauper who becomes a millionaire can throw away his old torn clothing.

-30 June 2021-

Lesson 5

ACCEPT SRILA PRABHUPADA AND MAKE LIFE SUBLIME

~~~ ~~~ ~~~

Srimad Bhagavatam 4.14.17

Austin, Texas

Date: 26-AUG-2021

Om Namo Bhagavate Vasudevaya

[Gurudeva sings three times and devotees repeat]

Replace lower lust with higher lust

rājann asādhv-amātyebhyaś
corādibhyaḥ prajā nṛpaḥ
rakṣan yathā baliṁ gṛhṇann
iha pretya ca modate

Synonyms

rājan — O King; *asādhu* —
mischievous; *amātyebhyaḥ* — from ministers; *cora-*
ādibhyaḥ — from thieves and rogues; *prajāḥ* — the
citizens; *nṛpaḥ* — the king; *rakṣan* —
protecting; *yathā* — accordingly as; *balim* —

taxes; *gṛhṇan* — accepting; *iha* — in this
world; *pretya* — after death; *ca* — also; *modate* —
enjoys.

Translation

The saintly persons continued: When the king protects the
citizens from the disturbances of mischievous ministers as
well as from thieves and rogues, he can, by virtue of such
pious activities, accept taxes given by his subjects. Thus
a pious king can certainly enjoy himself in this world as
well as in the life after death.

Purport

The duty of a pious king is described very nicely in this
verse. His first and foremost duty is to give protection to
the citizens from thieves and rogues as well as from
ministers who are no better than thieves and rogues.
Formerly, ministers were appointed by the king and were
not elected. Consequently, if the king was not very pious
or strict, the ministers would become thieves and rogues
and exploit the innocent citizens. It is the king's duty to
see that there is no increase of thieves and rogues either
in the government secretariat or in the departments of
public affairs. If a king cannot give protection to citizens
from thieves and rogues both in the government service
and in public affairs, he has no right to exact taxes from
them. In other words, the king or the government that
taxes can levy taxes from the citizens only if the king or
government is able to give protection to the citizens from
thieves and rogues.

In the Twelfth Canto of *Śrīmad-Bhāgavatam* (12.1.40) there is a description of these thieves and rogues in government service. As stated, *prajās te bhakṣayiṣyanti mlecchā rājanya - rūpiṇaḥ:* "These proud *mlecchas* [persons who are less than *śūdras*], representing themselves as kings, will tyrannize their subjects, and their subjects, on the other hand, will cultivate the most vicious practices. Thus practicing evil habits and behaving foolishly, the subjects will be like their rulers." The idea is that in the democratic days of Kali-yuga, the general population will fall down to the standard of *śūdras*. As stated (*kalau śūdra-sambhavaḥ*), practically the whole population of the world will be *śūdra*. A *śūdra* is a fourth-class man who is only fit to work for the three higher social castes. Being fourth-class men, *śūdras* are not very intelligent. Since the population is fallen in these democratic days, they can only elect a person in their category, but a government cannot run very well when it is run by *śūdras*. The second class of men, known as *kṣatriyas,* are especially meant for governing a country under the direction of saintly persons (*brāhmaṇas*) who are supposed to be very intelligent. In other ages — in Satya-yuga, Tretā-yuga and Dvāpara-yuga — the general populace was not so degraded, and the head of government was never elected. The king was the supreme executive personality, and if he caught any ministers stealing like thieves and rogues, he would at once have them killed or dismissed from service. As it was the duty of the king to kill thieves and rogues, it was similarly his duty to immediately kill dishonest ministers in government service. By such strict vigilance, the king could run the government very well, and the citizens would be happy to have such a king. The conclusion is that unless the king is perfectly able to give protection to the citizens from rogues and thieves, he has no right to levy taxes from the citizens for his own sense gratification. However, if he gives all protection to the citizens and levies taxes on them, he can live very happily and peacefully in this life, and at the end of this life be elevated to the heavenly kingdom or even to the Vaikuṇṭhas, where he will be happy in all respects. (End of purport)

Sankarshan das Adhikari:

This idea of protesting against the government is actually a proper mentality. I remember when I grew up the mood of the people of this country then was, they had come out of the World War II and they were very dedicated to the US government but the youth they were called baby boomers, we were born after the World War II. The baby boomers those who were born after the World War II grew up with a different mentality, because we were seeing so many faults and so protesting against the government was considered a very proper thing to do and that was actually setting the stage for Prabhupada to come to give the actual protest.

Here Prabhupada is giving the actual understanding of what is proper government. The proper government actually is the king. The king is the well-wisher of all the citizens. He makes sure there are no thieves and rogues, he can even kill them. He does not have to go to some trial or something, he can immediately kill. Nowadays, you can be a murderer and if you have enough money, you can appeal your conviction you can be postponed. You can sit in the prison for many, many years and not face capital punishment. We see it all the time, murderers are sitting and waiting for capital punishment for twenty years before they are executed.

In the Vedic culture, immediately, right on the spot kill him, no trial, no judge, no jury, and the king himself is the perfect judge. Who is proper and who is improper, he immediately kills them. Those rascals, in that way, the thieves and rogues were curbed down.

Here there are so many thieves and rogues, thousands and millions of thieves and rogues all over the world, cheating in this way, cheating in that way, cheating and cheating and cheating. In fact, modern-day society is called the society of the cheaters and the cheated. Everybody was trying to cheat us, but we only found one person who wasn't trying to cheat us and that was Srila Prabhupada. The whole world is full of cheaters, everybody is cheating. For their own selfish greedy, lusty, lazy purposes everyone is motivated. "What's in it for me" they have a saying. They don't recognize it because they don't think "God is number one" they think "I am number one. I am the centre; everything should be for my pleasure and should satisfy me". It is just like barking dogs, you get near their yard woof, woof, woof. These people are just like barking dogs. The whole society is like barking dogs.

So, we are very fortunate that we are blessed by a great pure devotee who was actually sent by Krishna. These books are directly ordered by God Himself, Krishna.

Krishna told Prabhupada that you go there and write those books, so these books are a very special thing. They are not some ordinary books. These books were ordered by God Himself. So when you pick up Prabhupada's books, you are connected with Srila Prabhupada, you are connected with Bhaktisiddhanta Sarasvati, Bhaktivinoda Thakkura, with six Goswamis, with Narada muni, you are connected with Radharani and Krishna and Lord Caitanya, just by touching these books and what to speak of reading them and trying to understand them. We have to learn how to see everything through the eyes of the books which is called *sastra caksus*, one who sees through the eyes of the scriptures. If your eyes are bad you will have to go to an optometrist and get some corrective lenses so you can see things as they are. In this age, we all have corrupted vision. We have polluted vision – polluted by lust, anger, greed, madness illusion, and envy. We can't see things as they are. But if we become *sastra caksus*, we see through the eyes of the scriptures then we can actually know things as they are. That's why these regular classes are very important. Prabhupada introduced Bhagavatam classes every morning as a standard. Studying Bhagavatam is very important and we also read Caitanya Caritamrita, Nectar of Devotion, Teachings of Lord Caitanya, Upadeshamrita - Nectar of Instruction, Sri Upanishad, Easy Journey to other planets, we read all of Prabhupada's books, every book that Prabhupada has authored. We almost read every one of them. Every day I am reading Prabhupada's books. I am hearing the classes and I am doing reading on my own also because the more you can read these books and see through the eyes of these books, the more your vision becomes perfect. Because the trouble is we are very polluted. We think "I am this body", "I am white", "I am black", "I am American", "I am Indian", "I am Lithuanian", "I am male", "I am female", "I am 74 years old", "I am 25 years old" this is all illusion. We are actually eternal spiritual beings qualitatively one with the Supreme Personality of Godhead.

> *īśvarah paramah Krsnah*
> *sac-cid-ānanda-vigrahah*
> *anādir ādir govindah*
> *sarva-kārana-kāranam*

Krsna who is known as Govinda is the Supreme Godhead. He has an eternal blissful spiritual body. He is the origin of all. He has no other origin and He is the prime cause of all causes.

Since we are being part and parcel of Him, we are qualitatively one with Him. Just like the same percentage of chemicals we find in the entire ocean, we find in the drop. Qualitatively they are the same thing, the same percentage of chemicals we find in the total ocean, we find in the drop of an ocean. Since Krishna has the qualities of eternity, knowledge, and bliss, we also have the qualities of eternity, knowledge, and bliss the only difference is the quantity. Krishna is infinite and we are infinitesimal that's the difference. Everything that exists is non-different from Krishna. Just like the sun and the sunshine, the sun is spread all over the universe in the form of sunshine. We even sing in the song "here comes the sun" the popular song of the Beatles here comes the sun, was that the sun planet? No. They wouldn't be singing, they would be dead if the sun planet would have come here but the sunshine came. So the sunshine is also considered the sun. So, the energy of Krishna is also considered Krishna. That's why Prabhupada taught us, the first lecture I heard in San Francisco was so nice. Prabhupada said that every day you are seeing the sun and the moon. Krishna says, "I am light of the sun and the moon". He says, "every time you drink water – once, twice, thrice, you remember Krishna is the taste of water." Then you immediately become Krishna conscious. To become Krishna conscious is not difficult, it simply requires practice.

So I lay down at night in my bedroom and I look out the window and there is the moon, shashi suryayoh – I am light of the sun and the moon. So, learn how to experience Krishna everywhere because Krishna is everywhere. He is in the form of Deity, He is in the form of His Names, He is in the form of prasadam, He is in the form of the Bhagavad-gita, Srimad Bhagavatam, He is in the form of a spiritual master; the external manifestation of the Supersoul. So, learn how to connect with Krishna unlimitedly. That's the key. From the moment you wake up till the moment you go to bed at night, you practice during the day then at night you dream about Krishna also. Just like Gurumataji told me that she had a dream yesterday. She told me in her dream there were Radha and Krishna Deities. Because she is so absorbed in serving Krishna 24 hours a day so when she dreams, she is also dreaming about Radha and Krishna. We can learn a lot from Gurumataji, she is a very advanced Vaishnavi, she really earns the name Gurumataji. She is definitely gurumataji.

If we take this process seriously then our lives will be sublime, we can become sober. That's what the first instruction I got when I was just coming around. I had not joined yet but I was attracted and Vishnujan swami said, "you have to become sober." He said in such a way it went in a deep, deep, deep, you have to become sober.

So, we have to give up being intoxicated by the material nature, by the opposite sex, by pleasures of the tongue and the genitals. We have to give up this intoxication. We should have one intoxication only and that is the holy Name, *Hare Krishna, Hare Krishna, Krishna Krishna, Hare Hare/ Hare Rama, Hare Rama, Rama Rama Hare Hare*. Let me become absolutely and totally intoxicated with the nectar of *Hare Krishna, Hare Krishna, Krishna Krishna, Hare Hare/ Hare Rama, Hare Rama, Rama Rama Hare Hare.* Even one syllable of the Hare Krishna mantra has so much nectar and can fill up millions and billions and trillions and quadrillions of universes still it has more volumes. We just have to learn how to connect with the holy names, that's why we seriously chant 16 rounds of Japa every day. Japa is not something "oh I got to nish nish nama nama get it done, finish, but no. Japa is the most important thing we do every day. Now how am I going to connect with Him? Am I just going to keep it on the tongue only, nish nish nam nama or I am going to take it deep, deep into my heart and let Krishna and Radharani dance in my heart. *Hare Krishna, Hare Krishna, Krishna Krishna, Hare Hare/ Hare Rama, Hare Rama, Rama Rama Hare Hare.* You have a choice of how seriously you are going to take this process. You can take it lightly or you can take it with the utmost seriousness with the understanding that you can die at any time.

A few days back I came close to death. Somehow Krishna kept me here, it was a very sobering thing that to go unconscious in my office and wake up in an ambulance. It was very sobering to have such an experience, To understand that I can die at any time, so let me become perfect now in Krishna consciousness, so I can carry out the order of my spiritual master to become a guru and deliver the world. I must take it very seriously. I have to become very serious, at every thought, with every word, with every deed in all times, places, and circumstances. I should be absolutely totally dedicated to Srila Prabhupada and previous acaryas, so that I can act perfectly as an instrument in the hands of my beloved Guru Maharaja for bringing the spiritual revolution to this planet as soon as possible.

There is no other solution. Right now, the whole planet is ruled by these damn demons, damn rascals. Just like the supreme court they had little intelligence here to make abortion illegal. But the president is trying to get around the supreme court ruling to keep abortion legal, the so-called president is killing innocent children, and he is in favor of murderess of innocent children, just see the so-called president of the United States. So the whole world is very much tortured and perplexed by the rascal baby killers, cow killers, and so-called leaders who are no better than man-eating rakshasas.

It is our duty to try to become pure devotees of Krishna and to spread pure devotion of Krishna as much as possible, bringing it back in every situation. Let me be in the mood of purely serving my spiritual master and Krishna in the mood of inspiring others to be pure devotees of guru and Krishna, wherever I go in all situations, always bringing it back to the point.

yato yato niścalati
manaś cañcalam asthiram
tatas tato niyamyaitad
ātmany eva vaśaṁ nayet

From wherever the mind wanders due to its flickering and unsteady nature, one must certainly withdraw it and bring it back under the control of the Self.

We have to get back, we have to get back, we have to get back, where we actually belong. We don't belong in the clutches of maya. We don't belong under Durga's jurisdiction. Durga is the prison keeper. We don't belong as prisoners of Durga devi.

sṛṣṭi-sthiti-pralaya-sādhana-śaktir ekā
chāyeva yasya bhuvanāni bibharti durgā
icchānurūpam api yasya ca ceṣṭate sā
govindam ādi-puruṣaṁ tam ahaṁ bhajāmi

The external potency Māyā who is of the nature of the shadow of the cit potency is worshiped by all people as Durgā, the creating, preserving, and destroying agency of this mundane world. I adore the primeval Lord Govinda in accordance with whose will Durgā conducts herself.

We don't want to remain as prisoners of Durga Devi, caught up here in the cycle of birth and death, and get carried away by lust, anger and greed, madness, illusion, and envy. We want to conquer the lower self by higher self. Actually, each one of us we are not of this material world. Do you realize that we are eternal associates of Krishna in the spiritual world. You actually have a relationship with Krishna as a gopi, a gopa, a cow, a peacock in the mood of a friend, a parent, a girlfriend, or a boyfriend, you have an eternal relationship called rasa with Krishna. We don't try to jump artificially. But we leave that up to Krishna. We don't, oh, I have to be a gopi or I have to be a cowherd boy otherwise I am not interested. No. we don't make any conditions. We are in the mood of completely surrendering to Krishna. I belong to You, however way You want me to serve You. If You want me to be a rock, where You sit and take Your lunch every day, whatever You want me to do my Lord, I can be a rock, I can be a peacock, whatever You want me to be, however I can best, serve You and please You. That's our mood totally, completely surrendered to Krishna, not demanding this rasa or that rasa. We all have eternal relationship with Krishna in the spiritual world. We have rasa with Krishna.

But due to thinking about what it would be, if I was the Supreme, Krishna gave us the chance to explore our curiosity. To get it out of our system basically, He wants our total love and devotion. But love and devotion cannot be forced. We had a curiosity what it would be like if I was the centre of the existence. So okay, don't think that way, but if you really want to think that way, then I will let you try, you can try to be the centre of existence. The first birth we actually take is Brahma. Each one of us were the Lord of the entire universe. So, when we first entered this material world, we were the Lords of the entire universe. Can you imagine we were Brahma we had so many demigods reporting to us, we had a whole universe that we were the Lord of but we weren't satisfied in that way. Let me try to be Indra, try to be this, or try to be that, we came all the way from Indra down to *indragopa* germ trying to be happy in this way and that way for millions and billions and quadrillions of lifetimes we have been caught up here in this time space continuum.

But now somehow or other we got this most fortunate human form and we are most fortunate to have come in contact with the great realized soul who was sent by Krishna Himself to this material world to deliver us His Divine Grace om Visnu-pada paramahamsa parivrajakacarya astottar-sata srimad A C Bhaktivedanta tridandi Goswami Maharaja Prabhuapada was sent here to deliver us from this madness. We should take very seriously of this mercy of Srila Prabhupada his divine instruction his divine sanga and by associating with those who had his association, we also get his association. Just like when I connect with my godbrothers I feel it helps me to strengthen my connection with Prabhupada, not that I only care about Prabhupada and nobody else. The more we can appreciate the servants of the servants, of the servants, of the servants, of the servants of the bona fide spiritual master, the more we become dear to the bona fide spiritual master. And the more we become dear to the bona fide spiritual master, the more we become dear to Krishna. So, take this process that Prabhupada has given us in his books don't manufacture your own new version of how to be Krishna conscious, oh, I will think of little sense gratification is ok I will mix in with little sense gratification here, some sense gratifications there, no, don't cheat yourself while trying to water down this process. Take it in its original pure form. If you take the watered-down version, you are not going to get free from lust, anger and greed, madness, illusion, and envy. Take the full version that Prabhupada is giving us without any pollution or distortion. Take it exactly as Prabhupada has given us and your life would be unbelievably sublime.

Devotee: How to keep mind pure and free from lusty thoughts.

SDA: By keeping it fixed in Krishna.

yato yato niścalati
manaś cañcalam asthiram

From wherever the mind wanders due to its flickering and unsteady nature, one must certainly withdraw it and bring it back under the control of the Self. Always keep bringing the mind back to Krishna. There are so many ways you can see the picture of Krishna; you can read a verse. You can memorize a verse. You can chant a verse. You can sing a bhajan. Just like there is a beautiful bhajan that I learned many years ago that Prabhupada sings and I often sing it during the morning program, while I am doing the services getting things ready to go on altar, I just start singing the bhajan by Narottam.

'gaurāṅga' bolite habe pulaka-śarīra
'hari hari' bolite nayane ba' be nīra.

That way, to me just doing the services is not enough, my mind could be thinking of nonsense while I am doing services, so I just sing some bhajans also when I dress the Deities also. There is also a beautiful song about the holy places of Vrindavan. Every day when I sit down to bathe Prabhupada, I not only bathe Prabhupada, but I sing this bhajan.

jaya rādhe, jaya kṛṣṇa, jaya vṛndāvan
śrī govinda, gopīnātha, madana-mohan

I sing the whole bhajan everyday when I am bathing Prabhupada. We have to do everything we can, engage in devotional service, chant and sing bhajans, chant some verses. Just like everyday, I like to chant Brahma Samhita prayers – the Govinda prayers. Those prayers are very nice. They are very powerful. Just like the one-

ānanda-cinmaya-rasātmatayā manaḥsu
yaḥ prāṇināṁ pratiphalan smaratām upetya
līlāyitena bhuvanāni jayaty ajasram-
govindam ādi-puruṣaṁ tam ahaṁ bhajāmi

I worship Govinda, the primeval Lord, whose glory ever triumphantly dominates the mundane world by the activity of His own pastimes, being reflected in the mind of recollecting souls as the transcendental entity of ever-blissful cognitive rasa.

So Krishna Prema, do you want to be one of those recollecting soul where Krishna did this, Krishna did that, Krishna said this. Because of His loving affection for Arjuna, Krishna broke His promise. He said, "I will not take part in the fight, I will be just your charioteer". But when Bhismadeva was instigated by Duryodhana that you must kill Arjuna, He said, "Yes, I will do it", but then Krishna had to break His promise. For Krishna, even His promise is less important in protecting His devotees. Just see the love and affection that Krishna has for His devotees, that He had to break His promise to protect His devotee.

Just think about these glorious pastimes of Krishna. I always think about this pastime and that pastime, sometimes if we don't have enough memory, then read the Krishna book, cover to cover, this pastime, that pastime, so many lilas, the Damodar lila bound with the ropes, and there are pastimes with the Deities also. You can meditate on Deities pastimes also because the Deities are also Krishna.

The original Damodara in ISKCON, there is a very interesting lila. There was a traveling Rock concert and they had the school bus, it was kind of bouncy and they had very beautiful Deities of Radha and Krishna, but to keep the Deities from falling down when they are bouncing up, they tied Him with ropes. When Prabhupada heard, "oh, they are tying Krishna with ropes" then Prabhupada said, "you can name that naughty boy Damodara from today". Prabhupada can call Him a naughty boy. So this is a pastime. And these Deities we have, they are named after. Those became personal Deities of Radha-Damodara traveling Sankirtan party of Vishnujan swami and Tamal Krishna Goswami and then later on, Tamal Krishna Goswami was blessed with finding this Deity on Juhu beach on the morning walk. One day, the tide was very far out to the sea, he noticed there was something shining in the sandy center. The devotee went and picked it up. It was the Deity of Krishna, so he named it after the original Radha-Damodara traveling Sankirtan party and we have them. Just meditating on this pastime of Damodara, it is the lila of Krishna. The lila of the Deity and the lila of Krishna Himself in the spiritual world is one and the same. So there are so many ways you can absorb your mind in Krishna conscious thoughts, pastimes, teachings, verses.

You can think of how I can do my duty to deliver the world. What can I do to be the deliverer of this world. That's the order Prabhupada gave us. How can think, speak, and act in such a way 24 hours a day, that I can become empowered in delivering the world. Start meditating like that, in that way you can keep yourself totally plugged into Krishna conscious 24 hours a day, and who needs low level lust. Low level lust means making a woman pregnant. But what's more loving – making one woman pregnant or making the whole world pregnant. Who needs the sex of the genitals? We have the supreme sex life that is preaching. Instead of injecting semen in some woman's womb, why not inject Krishna katha into the ears of the conditioned souls, that's even more powerful than sex life. This preaching is the ultimate sex because by preaching you can make the whole world pregnant. Why only make one woman pregnant, make the whole world pregnant. Why not go to the supreme lust. In that way, you can give up the lower lust and exchange it for the higher lust. I want to make the whole world pregnant. Supreme sex life is making the whole world pregnant with Krishna consciousness.

Raghunandan das: Nowadays, we don't have kings but a democratic form of government, then how do we ensure that we elect the right leaders when most of the population is ignorant and try to vote for the leaders who are ready to satisfy their desires?

SDA: We have to educate the voters, that's all we can do. The only hope is to make the voters Krishna conscious. They won't vote for anybody unless he is Krishna conscious. Right now, the population, because they are sudras they will vote for sudras. We have to make them Krishna conscious, then they will vote for Krishna conscious leaders. They go to the poll to find out if any devotee is running for any offices, if not then forget it, I am not voting, that should be the mood. Actually, one time in ISKCON we had a political party called "In God we trust", we had devotees running for office in Gainesville FL. Our temple president was running for the city council. But it is illegal for a religious organization to engage in politics. It is against the law. So, we had to stop it. But any devotees, who are on their own and they want to run for office here in Austin, I will definitely go vote for you. Of course, I can't vote in other places. If some devotees want to try running for office, so we can introduce Krishna conscious principles in the government. Devotees there, should definitely vote for him.

Devotee: Hare Krishna Srila Gurudeva! Dandavat Pranam! First of all, I want to say I am sorry because I confused with when you asked me to read. I am really very sorry for that. My question is how to take the process of Krishna consciousness seriously?

SDA: How to take it seriously, it is a very nice question. One thing I was blessed the other day by coming apparently it could have been death itself. I felt unconscious, I had to go to the hospital emergency room. When you understand that let me take it very seriously now myself. I was already taking it very seriously but now it is much more serious. I was thinking that maybe I got 20 more years, but I think at 74, I can die at any time. Of course, I am not, but my body is 74 years old. But you have to understand young people are dying all the time too. You can see everyday in the newspapers some young person died either it was by accident or something with their health problem. You have to understand at any moment death can come. So let me take it very seriously that at any moment I can leave this body. Let me train myself so when death comes, I can immediately say- Hare Krishna, and be qualified to go back to my original home in the spiritual world. Ok

Devotee: yes Gurudeva. Thank you so much.

SDA: You are welcome.

Sharada devi dasi: What helps me to be steady in the process.

SDA: You have taken initiation vows so you have to be honest. You have taken a vow so you have to keep your word otherwise you are like an animal. An animal can't take a vow and keep the promise. But as a human being, you have taken initiation vows, so now you have to live up to the vows you have taken. Everyday chant at least 16 rounds and give up illicit sex life, meat eating, intoxication, and gambling; become very serious. You can beg Krishna to help you. Krishna is right there with you at every minute, the spiritual master is also spiritually present at every minute. You can beg, "my dear spiritual master, my dear Srila Prabhupada, my dear Lord Caitanya, my dear Lord Nityananda, my dear Radha and Krishna, please bless me that I am having great difficulty to be steady in this process. So please help me." I am like a child learning to walk; I keep slipping and falling down along the way. I need to become strong and steady, every minute my mind is totally absorbed in loving service mood to Guru and Krishna. Please Guru Maharaja and Sri Krishna help me, so I can always be in this mood. Begging, begging, and begging; that's the key. You have to be in the mood of a beggar and always begging for the mercy, in that way, you will get the mercy. The more you beg for the mercy the more you will get the mercy. Don't think you are on your own, you can be Krishna conscious. Only by the mercy of guru and Krishna and Vaishnavas can you be Krishna conscious.

Aditya Raja: Maya distracts all people equally or she distracts devotees more.

SDA: No non-devotees are totally distracted. Devotees are less distracted and pure devotees are not at all distracted. The non-devotees are completely in maya's grip. The neophyte devotees are trying to go back and forth, back and forth, and fixed up devotees are almost completely fixed and pure devotees are totally fixed.

Dhiraj: What sort of relationship a soul can have with Krishna? Is it through both love and anger are acceptable forms of feelings.

SDA: No. Kamsa's mood is not in the spiritual world. He was inimical towards Krishna. Of course, mother Yashoda can be angry but her anger is in loving affection. She wants to train her boy to be a proper little boy. It is not biased, there can be anger in love, like she tied that little rascal with ropes, because He was naughty and to train that little naughty boy to be good, so she tied Him up with ropes. So that kind of divine anger could be but not inimical anger like Kamsa in the spiritual world.

I thank you all for tuning in. It is very nice that you all came.

Hare Krishna, Hare Krishna, Krishna Krishna, Hare Hare/ Hare Rama, Hare Rama, Rama Rama, Hare Hare.

ABOUT THE AUTHOR

His Grace Sriman Sankarshan Das Adhikari, is a practitioner and teacher of the science of Bhakti Yoga for over 50 years. He is an initiated disciple of His Divine Grace A.C. Bhaktivedanta Swami Prabhupada, the Founder Acharya of the International Society for Krishna Consciousness (ISKCON), from whom he has learned the topmost system of spiritual enlightenment, known as Krishna Consciousness or Bhakti Yoga.

By this process one can quickly and easily discern one's true spiritual eternal nature and come to understand the nature of God. Most significantly, one learns how to reciprocate in dealings of loving service with the Supreme Godhead. As one approaches this supreme stage of consciousness, one experiences higher and higher states of happiness culminating in unbounded bliss.

Before departing this world in 1977, Srila Prabhupada instructed Sriman Sankarshan Das Adhikari and his other disciples to take up his mission of propagating the ultimate science of Bhakti throughout the whole world for the benefit of all suffering humanity.

In obedience to Srila Prabhupada, Sankarshan Das Adhikari has fully taken up the banner of pure devotional service to the Supreme Godhead and made it his life's mission to spread the Krishna consciousness science as far and wide as possible throughout the world. In the year 2000, in reconfirmation of his spiritual master's order, he received the blessings of ISKCON's Governing Body Commission (GBC) to make disciples all over the world.

Though headquartered at Bhaktivedanta Ashram in Austin, Texas, USA, he regularly travels throughout the globe with his wife, Her Grace Srimati Vishnupriya Mataji, giving lectures on pure devotional service, enlivening and enlightening his varied audiences with this supreme knowledge, which has been so kindly bestowed upon him by his spiritual master. Thus, he regularly travels to all 6 inhabited continents on the planet, for over 7 months a year, to meet with his students and disciples to share the innermost secrets of how to perfect one's consciousness.

As a means to reach the most people across all boundaries of nationality, race, or creed, he has made this supreme knowledge freely available over the Internet through his e-course, "The Ultimate Self-Realization Course"™. As an adjunct to this course his realizations and selected correspondence are also made available via "Thought for the Day", an e-zine, which is sent daily via the Internet to inspire and guide his thousands of students around the globe.

Most importantly, he makes himself completely available to his students and disciples for consultation and guidance, through emails, phone calls or face-to-face meetings. All free of charge.

"This supreme divine consciousness is already present within each one of us at this very moment!" he explains. "We just have to reawaken our dormant Krishna Consciousness or God Consciousness within our heart, by taking the perfect instructions of the bona fide spiritual master. Just like fire is present within a match. All it takes is for someone to strike the dry match on a striking surface and the fire within the match will become manifest."

Thus, lighting the torch of divine knowledge in the hearts of his audience, relieving their material suffering through his devotional music, his lectures, and most of all through his personal contact, this spiritual teacher is committed to nothing less than revolutionizing the consciousness of the entire world!

Printed in Great Britain
by Amazon

25755852R00069